MOTHER-INFANT INTERACTION

MOTHER-INFANT INTERACTION

Edited by

C. Etta Walters

HUMAN SCIENCES PRESS
SUBSIDIARY OF BEHAVIORAL PUBLICATIONS INC.
72 FIFTH AVENUE, NEW YORK, N.Y. 10011

Library of Congress Catalog Number 74-12621
ISBN: 0-87705-240-9 clothbound
0-87705-284-0 paperback

Copyright © 1976 by Human Sciences Press, a division
of Behavioral Publications, Inc., 72 Fifth Avenue, New
York, New York 10011

Printed in the United States of America
56789   987654321

COVER DESIGN: LYNN J. HOLLYN
PHOTOGRAPH: VINCENT M. CACICIO

To the memory of my mother

CONTRIBUTORS

Julinda Abu Nasr, *Ph.D.*
Beirut University College
Beirut, Lebanon

Moon-Hi Ro, *Ph.D.*
Florida State University
Tallahassee, Florida

Cecile C. Baker, *Ph.D.*
Division of Mental Health
State of Florida
Tallahassee, Florida

Betty J. Stewart, *Ph.D.*
Division of Mental Health
State of Louisiana
Baton Rouge, Louisiana

Clayton E. Stumpff, *M.S.*
Urban League Child Care Center
Colorado Springs, Colorado

Joseph E. Crum, *Ph.D.*
Child Guidance Clinic of
 Pinellas County
St. Petersburg, Florida

C. Etta Walters, *Ph.D.*
Florida State University
Tallahassee, Florida

Howard Protinsky, *Ph.D.*
Virginia Polytechnic Institute
Blacksford, Virginia

Patricia Wilhoit, *M.S.*
Tallahassee Community College
Tallahassee, Florida

CONTENTS

EDITOR'S NOTE

This book discusses mother-infant interaction in the emotional, social, and perceptual-cognitive areas of development. Each of the three areas consists of three chapters, each dealing with different aspects of development in that domain. Special emphasis is placed on the importance of mother-infant interaction during the first eighteen months of life. The various authors of these chapters present time-tested findings as well as recent research studies pertaining to the topic under discussion.

INTRODUCTION

If you love it,
Let it go free.
If it returns,
It is yours.
If not,
It never was.

Anonymous

The uniqueness of each person is evident at birth. In his physiological functioning and his neurological makeup, reflected dramatically at this stage by his sensitivity to stimuli, every individual reveals his distinctiveness from the start.

While the length and breadth of potential development in the emotional and intellectual spheres are constitutionally set at birth, the role of the mother[1] must not be underestimated. The well-known English child analyst D. W. Winnicott (1960) has made the important point that the "inherited potential of the infant cannot be-

---

1. "Mother" refers throughout the book not only to the biological mother but also to the caretaking mother or surrogate.

come an infant unless linked to maternal
care" (p. 94).

The seeds of good mothering lie in
the background, genetic and environmental,
of the potential mother and are nurtured
in the dark waters of the womb. In this
uterine environment, the relationship of
the fetus with the mother is a parasitic
one, based on total physiological dependency and fusion. Even at this age the fetus can experience intrauterine distress
from such sources as cord strangulation or
emotional trauma of the mother.

This relationship is abruptly ter-
minated at birth; but, as Freud (1926) has
written, there is a greater continuity between prenatal life and earliest infancy
than the birth process might indicate.
From intrauterine biological dependency
upon the mother, the infant in the first
year of life passes on to a period of social symbiosis with his mother. It is not
until the next period that he develops social interrelationships.

Spitz (1965) has listed some of the
unique aspects of this early mother-infant
relationship as follows:

1. The psychic structure of the two
differ.

2. The relationship will not be one
of equal dependency, and the contributions of each in this mutual relationship
will be dissimilar.

3. The adult's personality structure
is well developed and defined, whereas the
opposite is true of the newborn.

4. The environment of the two is

vastly different in that the adult has had
many persons and activities in his life,
while the newborn has but one single individual. Even in this relationahip the
mother is not seen as separate from himself.

5. While the child's total environment includes the family setting, these
environmental influences are transferred
to the child by the one who gratifies his
needs--that is, his mother.

It is important, therefore, to study
the personality of both mother and infant
and the ways in which they interact with
each other, keeping in mind that both can
be instigators of acts as well as reactors.
While from birth the infant is dependent upon an object (his mother) for survival and gratification, it is not until
the second half of the first year that he
develops object relations.
The infant's biological dependence
has evolved to one of both biological and
psychological dependence. The mother who
is the infant's first object of identification (A. Freud 1971) is now seen as
separate from the infant. In addition to
the baby recognizing her as a need-grati-
fying agent, he also desires her love;
she has become his libidinal-object and
the infant has now developed object relations.
Although the baby does not develop
object relations until approximately
five months and beyond, he has laid down
memory traces of experiences involving
maternal care and his own body and psychic self in the first several months
(Jacobson 1964). Jacobson believes that

mother and infant become tuned in to each other as early as the first few weeks of life.

A mother who is sensitive to her infant's needs evokes pleasurable feelings in the baby and from this the baby develops love for his mother. Spitz (1965) has written: "All later relations with object quality, the love relation, ... and ultimately all interpersonal relations have their first origin in the mother-child relation" (p. 296).

This book is an attempt to explore and explain the beginnings, ramifications, and implications of the all-important and all pervasive tie between mother and infant--truly the tie that binds.

PART I

EMOTIONAL DEVELOPMENT

This section is concerned with mother-infant interaction and how it affects the emotional development of the infant. Dr. Stewart concentrates on the early mother-infant care unit and how it influences ego development and object relations. She ties this in with some of the pathological manifestations of inadequate maternal care. Dr. Walters deals with the maternal relations, as well as the constitutional factors, which influence infant security. She brings to the reader recent empirical documentation of some of the later correlates of infant security. Dr. Protinsky reviews the literature dealing with the many factors involved in the part mother-infant relations play in the etiology of psyco-pathology.

INTRODUCTION TO PART I

C. Etta Walters

> The longing to return to or to
> retain the early symbiotic rela-
> tionship with the mother probably
> never ceases to play a role in our
> emotional life.
>
> *Anonymous*

Emotional experiences find their first
expressions in bodily--somatic and visceral
--reactions. This is true not only of the
neonate and young infant but apparently
also of the fetus (Greenacre 1941; Greene
1958; Sontag 1944). While these experiences
are no doubt without psychic content in the
fetus and young infant, they nonetheless
leave their impressions and effects.

Early affective responses exist at the
unconscious and autonomic level. MacLean
(1949), in reviewing recent evidence for
Papez's proposed theory of emotions, has
termed the phylogenetically old brain--the
rhinencephalon--the "visceral brain." He
makes the following points: the rhinen-
cephalon deals largely with visceral and
emotional factors; it is strategically

9

located to relate internal and external
perceptions; and it has many connections
with the hypothalamus to facilitate discharge of its impressions.

This primitive brain, lacking cortical control, operates at a symbolic and
nonverbal level. Because it does not have
the intellectual and/or verbal ability of
the neocortex, it remains at the mercy of
a variety of diffuse and unrelated stimuli
and discharges its impressions indiscrimi-
nately into the hypothalamus and lower
centers. MacLean points out how this may
lead to a "variety of ridiculous correlations leading to phobias, obsessive-com-
pulsive behaviors, etc." (p. 200).

According to MacLean, the infant's
preoccupation with feeding may lead him
to symbolically equate being fed in a satisfactory and loving atmosphere with emotional security. Conversely, not obtain-
ing relief with feeding could give rise
to feelings of insecurity, resentment, and
hostility. This theory might also explain
how an infant being adequately fed nutri-
tionally, but in an atmosphere associated
with harsh words or looks, could react
with visceral aggression.

MacLean suggests that patterns of
emotional behavior resulting in excessive and abnormal visceral responses and
repeated often enough might become per-
manently fixed in the visceral brain and
thus perpetuated into adult life. He says
psychosomatic patients lack the ability
to verbalize their emotions; this may be
because their emotional feelings originat-
ing in the hippocampal formation are immediately discharged into their autonomic
centers instead of going to the cerebral
cortex for scrutiny. He remarks, "This

situation helps explain the difference
between what we 'feel' and what we 'know'"
(p. 348).

Along the same line of thinking,
Spitz (1965) believes the newborn infant
at first *receives* rather than *perceives*
stimuli, and this reception is centered
in the autonomic nervous system. It is
primarily visceral and is expressed in
terms of emotions. Spitz terms this original reception of stimuli a "coenesthetic
organization." These first sensory impressions are diffuse, nonlocalized, and mostly visceral. The neonate and young infant
experience oral, skin, and vestibular sensations as a total proprioceptive impression, which is mediated through contact.

Spitz (1955) has written eloquently
of his thesis that all perception begins
in the oral cavity, and he sees the mouth
as serving both inner reception and external perception. As such, the mouth
forms the "cradle of perception" (Spitz
1965). He also sees this nonverbal type
of perception associated with the feeding
process. He says in the nursing process
three organs are involved in contact perception: the hand, the labyrinth, and the
outer skin. He sees these all fused into
one perceptual experience:

> When the child is lifted and cradled
> in the mother's arms, pressed against
> her body and held securely during the
> act of nursing, it comes near to the
> blissful intrauterine state in which
> need tension never arose and the in-
> security of our modern baby cot with
> its lack of support was unknown
> (Spitz 1955, p. 227).

The coenesthetic organization that exists at birth gradually evolves to what Spitz has called the "diacritic organization"--sensations localized and centered in the cortex; still, for the first five to six months, the infant is controlled predominately by the coenesthetic structure.

Despite the fact that the infant's eyes and ears are functioning as transducers soon after birth, "diacritic vision and audition do not appear to be used by the newborn child for the purposes of differentiating himself from his environment" (Freedman 1972, p. 366). Visual stimulation for the first five to six months appears to be experienced as a part of the coenesthetic organization.

Freedman has cited animal studies to develop his hypothesis that early deficient coenesthetic input in humans appears to end in irreversible emotional and ego deficits. He attributes the larger per cent of congenitally blind infants who develop autism--approximately 25 percent as compared to less than 1 per cent in the sighted population (Fraiberg and Freedman 1964)--to the lesser amount of coenesthetic stimulation some receive. Very frequently blind infants are referred to as "very good babies" who do not demand attention; hence they may not have adequate stimulation.

In seeking an explanation for why children from the same environment and with the same genetic endowment will differ in their emotional development, Freedman relies on Escalona's (1965) discussion of the interaction of the individual and his environment.

Escalona has written about the "organismic state," an active process depending upon the individual's present state of maturation, his past experiences, and his present physiological state. At any given time, the organismic state interacts with the environment to effect an intervening variable that Escalona terms a "pattern of concrete experience." The individual then makes adjustments, or adaptations, to this pattern of concrete experience, and a new organismic state emerges. Freedman believes it may be possible--say in the case of the blind infant--to make adjustments in the environment that will compensate for the organismic factor and produce patterns of concrete experience compatible with that of the normally developing infant.

Spitz (1965) has reminded us that the frightening explosive emotion of the adult that may occur in times of extreme stress is nothing more than the coenesthetic organization breaking through the barriers of the rational control of the diacritic organization. When we see such emotion in the infant, we tend to think this is part of his being an infant. However, this is not so, says Spitz; and we should view it as anything but trifling.

It seems, therefore, that to whatever orientation one subscribes regarding the genesis of psychopathology, there is a general agreement that it is related to early parent-child relationships, especially those with the mother.

1. MOTHER-INFANT CARE UNIT

Betty J. Stewart

> Object relationships do not mature
> into object constancy unless the
> child's first loved figures remain
> stable.
>
> A. Freud (1968)

There is no such thing as an infant.
Whenever one finds an infant, one finds maternal care; and without maternal care,
there would be no infant (Winnicott 1960).
In spite of the unitary nature of infant
and mother, however, the idea that infants
need a continuous and emotionally satisfying relationship with one person has been
explicit in the literature for only a short
time (Brody 1956). It derived from observations of infants separated from their mothers by necessity--that is, orphans and
those placed in institutions during war-
time. Investigators like Ribble and Spitz
called attention to the effects on infants
of maternal deprivation by describing instances of "marasmus," or wasting away for
no physiological cause, and "anaclytic depression," a reaction to separation from

the mother bringing about the gross arrest of the infant's ego development. Psychoanalytic theory maintains that experiences during the first year of life determine much of the developing child's capacity for healthy personality development.

In recent years there have been countless studies of infant-mother relationships and much new theory growing out of research findings. This chapter will attempt to examine current thinking concerning the tasks of the infant-maternal care unit in the first year of life and the importance of the relationship of mother and infant to each other.

PRENATAL INFLUENCES

Benedek (1956) emphasized that, for both infant and mother, developmental processes are intensively interactive and begin at conception. She suggested that the pregnant woman's feelings about herself and the developing infant color the relationship long before the baby is born. Alien emotional and environmental conditions, then, especially in the first trimester of pregnancy, may alter inner physiological and biochemical conditions so as to cause damage to the developing fetus.

Sontag (1944) in research at the Fels Institute reported that mothers undergoing severe emotional stress during pregnancy produce hyperactive, irritable infants with frequent gastrointestinal disturbances. He detected greatly increased fetal movements during periods of emotional stress and fatigue for the mother. In his opinion, these infants are already

neurotic at birth because of an unsatisfactory fetal environment.

Greenacre (1941) has theorized that
evidence points to the possible existence
of anxiety reactions of the fetus prior to
birth. She suggests that traumatic stimuli, such as loud noises, umbilical cord
entanglements, strong vibrations, and
other unknown uterine difficulties may
cause a predisposition to anxiety, much
stronger in some infants than in others.
She proposes:

> Where this predisposition to anxiety
> is great due to the overload of po-
> tential in prenatal, natal, or imme-
> diate postnatal experience, then new
> anxiety might pull down the whole
> load as it were, and by its peculiar
> paralyzing effect on the organism im-
> pair the sound synthesis of intro-
> jection and projection (p. 50).

This would prevent the developing recognition of the environment as separate from
the self.

This kind of anxiety, Greenacre (1941)
hypothesizes, precedes the anxiety pattern
established by birth trauma and probably
augments it. Her theory is based in part on
analytic work with adult neurotics who are
characterized by an unusual clairvoyant
quality. This quality, she feels, can be
observed in the tense, potentially anxious
infant who is the most sensitive reflector
of people around him. Greenacre theorizes
that this kind of anxiety leaves an organic
stamp, a kind of increased indelibility of
reaction to anxiety potential situations,
on the makeup of the child. In later life
it results in an increase in narcissism

and an insecure and easily slipping sense
of reality.
   Longitudinal studies by Thomas, et
al. (1970) of children from birth through
age fourteen have supported the idea that
infants are born with decidedly different
temperaments and begin to express themselves as individuals from birth. "Temperament" is defined as a child's individual
style of responding to the environment.
Thomas et al. propose that this distinct
individuality in temperament can be pro-
filed in the early weeks of an infant's
life and that it will persist as he grows
and develops, independently of the parents' handling or personality style.
   Thus the pregnant mother's emotional
life, activity level, and physical status
seem likely to contribute to the shaping
of the physical status, the behavior patterns, and the postnatal progress of the
child (Montagu 1965).

                BIRTH AND NORMAL AUTISM

   The birth process is the first real
separation of the infant from his mother.
In psychoanalytic theory it is seen as the
prototype of all human anxiety. All anxi-
ety-occasioning situations in later life
are thought to signify a separation from
the mother--first only biological, then as
a direct object loss, then of an object
less mediated in indirect ways (Greenacre 1941).
   The intrauterine, parasite-host
relationship which the fetus experiences
within the mother's body must be replaced
in the postnatal period by the enveloping

matrix of maternal care (Mahler 1968). The physiological symbiosis, abruptly termi- nated by the birth process, for the in- fant's survival must be replaced by what Mahler calls a "social symbiosis." The newborn's undifferentiated ego is comple- mented by psychobiological rapport between nursing--or bottle-feeding--mother and baby. Normal empathy on the part of the mother is the human substitute for in- stinct, which the animal relies on for survival (Mahler 1952).

According to Mahler, the infant does not move directly from prenatal symbiosis to social symbiosis but for the first few weeks seems to be in a state of hallucina- tory disorganization which she terms "nor- mal autism."

The infant's need at this time is to maintain homeostasis, or a steady state, and the mother's task is to help him with this. As hunger is relieved by feeding and discomfort becomes comfort, the infant be- gins to differentiate between pleasure and unpleasure and good and bad feelings. The rhythm of maternal movements associated with body warmth offers the infant a par- tial reinstatement of prenatal conditions and helps bridge the change from intra- mural to extramural life (Escalona 1963).

From about the second month, the in- fant behaves as though he and the mother are one, sharing the same boundary within which all his needs are met (Mahler 1968). This marks the beginning of Mahler's peri- od of social symbiosis.

SOCIAL SYMBIOSIS

Greenacre (1960) has described the mother-infant relationship during the first year as progressing in logical order. First there is the shift from an almost wholly mother-infant, biologically driven, relationship to a postnatal emotional relationship still dependent on physical and bodily contact. This, in turn, merges into the beginnings of a psychological relationship with feelings of mutual closeness and warmth. Following this, there comes the dawn of differentiation of the infant's self from the mother, a process dependent greatly on cooperation between the two. Along with this beginning capacity for object relationship comes the gradually increasing importance of the father in the life of the infant, the growing awareness not only of separateness from the mother but also from others, and the appreciation of the difference between others.

Within this framework the functions of the mother and the part the infant plays in the process are vital.

Winnicott (1960) has proposed that the mother's task is to help the infant journey from complete dependence to relative dependence to autonomy, or from the pleasure principle to the reality principle. The infant at birth contains within himself the tendency toward growth and development, but his "becoming" is linked to maternal care (Greenacre 1960).

Spitz (1965) sees the mother as the "auxiliary ego" of the infant. Winnicott (1960) has described the mother's role in terms of "holding," which is a total environmental provision that precedes "living with." The main function of this holding environment is the reduction to a minimum of impingements to which the infant must react. The mother serves as organizer and regulator of the infant's instinctual needs; how she influences the balance between discharge and maintenance of tension seems crucial to ego development (Ritvo and Solnit 1958). She must be both stimulus barrier and provider of needed stimulation.

Winnicott's "holding" is the mother's form of loving the infant. It should include not only physical closeness to the mother's body but the soft, pliable, cuddling touch of the mother (Erikson 1950; Greenacre 1960; Harlow 1958). The infant needs to be able to touch and feel differences of temperature, texture, and moistness, and to be saturated with comforting, familiar odors (Greenacre 1960). All of these ordinary kinds of experiences are necessary for the infant to begin to feel separate from the mother.

Mahler (1968) has suggested that the infant presents a variety of cues to the mother. The mother responds selectively to only certain of these cues. The infant gradually alters his behavior in relation to the selective response, and this circular interaction gives birth to the child's individual personality.

Greenacre (1960) has emphasized the importance of timing on the mother's part. She suggests that "marked and consistent maternal interference may result in impairment of sound ego development" (p. 581). Escalona (1963) has observed that the mother's manner of approaching the baby socially is most important. She ar-

gues that the infant's experience, and
hence his behavior, is determined by intrinsic and extrinsic factors--not to
varying proportions, but in interaction.
Winnicott (1960) sums up the results of reliable maternal care as follows:

1. The infant attains unit status--
he becomes an individual.

2. Linkage of motor, sensory, and
functional experiences occurs; that is,
the infant gains a psychosomatic existence.

3. There occurs the dawn of intelligence (vague beginnings of secondary
processes and symbolic functioning).

4. Fusion of aggressive and erotic
experiences takes place.

5. Object relations develop--infant
and mother are no longer merged--the "living in" stage begins.

Within the framework of the "holding
environment," the infant is not a passive
recipient. As mentioned above, he has a
temperament of his own and he tosses out
cues to his mother. Ritvo and Solnit
(1958) suggested that environmental influences may reinforce the infant's basic
predisposition, or they may conflict with
it. For example, frustration seems in-
evitable for the hyperactive infant with
a mother whose needs are for a passive
child, or for the baby whose need for tactile stimulation cannot be met by a mother
who becomes anxious at touching and hand-

ling.

Escalona (1963) has proposed that organismic characteristics such as activity
level or perceptual sensitivity may determine the impact of external stimulation
upon the child's experience. She found
that, with infants at six months, social
stimulation is a necessary condition for
the emergence of relatively mature behavior in motorically inactive babies; but
this is not the case for markedly active
babies.

Thomas et al. (1970) have recognized
that a maternal demand that conflicts ex-
cessively with temperamental characteristics and capacities is likely to place a
child under heavy and even unbearable
stress. Escalona (1967) has noted that
with progressive development, the infant,
left to himself, provides for himself the
kind of bodily sensations which the mother
has provided for him at moments of intense
and pleasurable interaction.

As mother and infant interact with
mutual satisfaction, the infant's ego
gains strength and attachment behavior can
be observed.

Attachment behavior is behavior
through which a discriminating, differential, affectional relationship
is established with a person or object, and which tends to evoke a
response from the object, and thus
initiates a chain of interaction
which serves to consolidate the
affectional relationship (Ainsworth
1964, p. 51).

Ainsworth found that attachment behavior passes through four main phases in

the first year of life. The first, that of undiscriminating responsiveness to people, occurs very early and seems related to tension relief. The second phase, occurring between eight and twelve weeks, shows some discrimination of the mother from other people as evidenced by differential crying and smiling. This would seem to coincide generally with the beginning of Mahler's "social symbiosis."

At about six months, the infant attempts to follow the mother. The third phase, beginning around six months of age, shows stronger attachment, protest at the mother's leaving, responsiveness to her return, and the use of the mother as a secure base from which to explore. The fourth phase occurs shortly after the baby shows a clearly defined attachment to the mother. He begins to attach himself to significant others and shows marked preference for certain people. Fear of strangers appears after the baby becomes discriminating in his attachments, often by the eighth month.

Overlapping with and paralleling attachment behavior is the development of person permanence and object permanence. Bell (1970) found that (1) babies tend to be more advanced in their concept of persons than in their concept of inanimate objects as permanent; (2) differences in the rate of development of person permanence are related to the quality of attachment behavior which a baby exhibits toward his mother; and (3) differences in the rate of development of person permanence can affect, in turn, the development of object permanence. Bell concludes that "the link between attachment and the development of person permanence is to be

found in the quality of mother-infant
interaction" (p. 308).

Ainsworth (1964) has noted again the
active part the infant himself plays in
the development of attachment behavior.
She believes that it is largely through
his own activity that the child becomes
attached, rather than through passive need
gratification or external stimulation.
Thus interaction between infant and mother
may be initiated by either the mother's
action, to which the baby responds, or by
the infant's cues, signals or overtures,
to which the mother responds. Maternal
deprivation, then, becomes not the absence
of a mother but the lack of interaction
between the infant and the mother.

The traditional game of peek-a-boo,
played naturally by mother with infant,
reflects and contributes to the development of object relations. As mutually responsive communication with a love object,
it offers the infant safe opportunity to
practice differences and fosters separation and individuation. The early stages
of the game can be called transitional,
halfway between autoerotic activity and
true object relations (Kleeman 1967).

SEPARATION-INDIVIDUATION

Both the development of discriminatory attachment behavior and person permanence imply that the infant has moved
from social symbiosis into the beginning
of a normal separation-individuation phase
of development. The mother's provision of
an adequate holding environment in which
she is responsive to the infant's needs

and cues makes separation possible. Winnicott (1960) notes that when maternal care
meets the specific and developing needs of
the infant, it is scarcely noticed. The
inherited potential gradually develops,
the ego gains strength, the infant experiences a continuity of being that readies
him for new developmental tasks. When
there is a failure of maternal care, ego-
annihilation at worst and severe impairment of ego development at best is the result.

Erikson (1963) has maintained that
the first year of life is a critical period for infant-mother relationship. He sees
the formation of basic trust as the first
developmental task of the ego and as one
that is vital to all future tasks. Because
the infant is totally dependent on maternal care, the establishment of basic trust
is a task for maternal care.

The kind of consistent mothering necessary for the development of object relations is also necessary for the formation
of trust. Trust seems to grow out of the
infant's conviction that his mother has
become "an inner certainty as well as an
outer predictability" (Erikson 1963, p.
247). Erikson says trust means trust in
others as well as a basic feeling of one's
own trustworthiness. The consistent meeting of the infant's needs that seems to
result in the development of trust again
depends on the quality of maternal care.

PATHOLOGY IN INFANCY

Much of the theory concerning normal
infant-mother relationship has derived

from the study of symptom pictures presented by children with psychoses (Mahler
1968). Spitz (1953) estimated that, aside
from factors like congenital disease and
physical interference, the psychological
influence on the child during infancy can
be reduced to what occurs in the mother-
infant relationship. Mahler maintains that
the main cause of "proclivity for aliena-
tion of the ego from reality and fragmen-
tation is a specific conflict of the mother-child relationship" (Mahler 1952, p.
294).

Nonetheless, Mahler has stated that
there are infants with inherently defec-
tive tension-regulating apparatuses which
probably cannot be complemented by either
the most quantitatively or qualitatively
efficient mothering. She maintains that it
is very difficult to ascertain whether severe psychiatric disturbance in infancy is
caused by the mother's pathology or lack
of empathy or the infant's great ego devi-
ation; that is, his inherent lack of contact with the living environment or in-
ordinate need for parasitic fusion with
the adult. She has observed many schizophrenic children whose mothers do not seem
to lack warmth, love, and genuine acceptance and who are not possessive, infan-
tilizing, or restrictive.

From the point of view of object relations development and the development of
a sense of reality, Mahler (1952) has
noted two groups of distrubed infants. In
one, the mother, as representative of the
outside world, seems never to have been
perceived emotionally by the infant. The
mother remains a part object; there is no
cathexis of infant energy to the mother.
This Mahler refers to as "infantile

autism."

In the other group, the infant's mental representation of the mother seems regressively fused with--not separated from-- the self. These infants seem to remain in a symbiotic relationship with the mother and to experience affective panic with separation. This Mahler terms "symbiotic infantile psychosis."

Spitz (1953) has observed that in physical illness compounded by the loss of the need-satisfying object, the separated infant cannot find a target for the discharge of his drive. He becomes tearful, demanding, and clinging in an attempt to regain the lost object with the help of his aggressive drive. After two months of uninterrupted separation, the infant seems to give up and shows definite somatic symptoms: sleeplessness, loss of appetite, loss of weight, and progressive deterioration. Spitz maintains that the infant thus turns aggression against himself. If the process is not interrupted, the result is death. Solnit (1969) notes that when hospitalized infants have developed symptoms of anaclytic depression and are then given large doses of substitute mothering, their first response of recovery and adaptation is an irritable, aggressive reaction. This, he feels, marks the redirection of aggressive energies to an external object.

The part that mismatching of mother and infant plays in severe infant disturbance is still unclear. Brody (1958) theorizes that subtle unresponsiveness or overresponsiveness of the mother may be the underlying cause in infant pathology; but she recognizes the difficulty of observing such interaction.

SUMMARY AND IMPLICATIONS

All of the research evidence explored
in this chapter points to the vital need
of every infant for quality maternal care
in order for healthy ego development to
occur. However, the maternal care-infant
relationship is both subtle and complex.
The best mothering seems to result from
having been well mothered.

Winnicott (1960) has observed that
perhaps the best way to help a mother provide a suitable holding environment is to
give her support. This would point to the
need for emotional feeding of the mother
from significant others.

As Wolfenstein (1953) has noted, parents cannot be taught the fundamentals of
child rearing in the same way that one
might teach them to repair a leaky faucet;
parents have unresolved childhood problems
and unconscious longings that serve as effective filters for what they hear. They
continue to meet their needs through their
children.

The emphasis from all theory and research findings that the key to infant-
mother interaction is quality mothering is
a painful reminder that there is no prescribed formula for quality mothering.
Perhaps most mothers do want to do the
very best for their infants and really
help with this vital task. New programs
that teach the principles we believe to be
essential ought to be easily available to
all mothers.

Another implication seems to be that
early identification of distrubed children
is essential. Usually it has been kinder-
garten or primary school teachers who have

called attention to them; this time is too late. Research findings indicate that the longer the child is immersed in a pathological situation, the poorer the chance is to provide therapeutic assistance.

Skolnick and Skolnick (1971) have suggested that the American nuclear family, in which the mother is confined with young children with no outside assistance, is a breeding ground for pathology. They assert that many, if not most, parents are unable to meet their children's needs because of their own personality problems. They suggest new forms of the family that would provide assistance and relief for both mothers and children.

Another proposed remedy is a network of day-care centers for young children. At least this could relieve overwhelmed mothers of a task they are ill prepared for and give infants and young children exposure to at least some consistent, positive, rewarding experiences.

Harlow (1966) has presented evidence that seems to point to the need for research in the area of mother surrogates and the possible therapeutic effects of siblings or other children in child-rearing practices.

In spite of the volume of theory and research in the area of infant-mother relationship, many questions remain unanswered. The field is fertile for new research.

INFANT SECURITY[1]

C. Etta Walters

> Through the rhythmic repetition of
> the gratification of his physiological
> needs, the infant develops to the
> perception that the source of the
> need (hunger, pain, discomfort) is
> within, and the source of gratifica-
> tion is outside the self.
>
> Benedek (1949)

The neonate and young infant's needs
lie in the realm of biological functioning
and are centered in feeding, sleeping,
elimination, relief from tension, and in

1. The data discussed in this study were
part of a longitudinal research project on
fetal activity and apprehension and aggression supported by a grant from the
National Institutes of Mental Health (Behavioral Science Research Branch) ROI MH
12831, 1966-71. Appreciation is extended
to Mrs. Barbara Orthner and Dr. Cheryl Mc-
Gahee for their assistance and dedication
to the study, and to the mothers and their
children who made the project possible.

maintaining homeostasis. The mother who responds to the infant's own special needs is laying the foundation for security.

The mother must do more than see that her baby is fed when hungry and comforted when distressed. She must learn to distinguish not only between his needs and desires (Weil 1970) but also between her own needs and those of the infant. Most importantly, her ministrations should be conducted in a sensitive and loving atmosphere.

The formation of structure depends upon rhythmic alternations of gratification and frustration experiences. The predictability of such a rhythm, associated with maternal love, prepares for the foundation of object constancy (Mahler 1963).

The neonate is completely dependent upon the mother for gratifications of needs; but excessive gratification can be harmful. All later forms of relationships will, in comparison, be disappointing (A. Freud 1971). By that same token, lack of satisfaction or excessive frustration results in a search for compensation, and the individual seeks libidinal investment in inanimate or animate objects only on a need basis. Anna Freud warns that we do not know if it is excessive frustration or excessive gratification in the first year that produces a selfish and promiscuous person.

Not only can frustrations and/or unrelieved tensions affect later psychological development but, depending upon the maturity of the vegetative nervous system and the gastrointestinal tract, they may become bound to parts of the gastrointestinal system and its actions (Benedek 1949). This may predispose the infant to later somatic complaints.

It would seem therefore that the pro-
totypes of ego constellations originate in
physiological functions and somatic affects (Spitz 1965). Especially important
is the satisfaction attained by all behaviors connected with feeding. Benedek
(1949) refers to Rado and Fenichel, who
pointed out that this satisfaction is the
first regulator of self-esteem. When feeding is unsatisfactory, they assume, "it
may cause a sense of helplessness, of in-
feriority, of worthlessness; as if 'bad-
ness' were existing within the self"
(Benedek, p. 652).

This chapter will deal with the
security findings that were a part of a
research project by the author. Results
of this study shed some light on maternal as well as prenatal and/or constitutional correlates of security.

Security, in this study, was measured
by the Flint Security Scale. Flint (1959)
developed an early infancy security scale
that is dependent on behavioral assess-
ments much as the Gesell Developmental
Schedules (1947) were. Flint studied data
reported by parents over several years.
She looked first for signs of independence, especially in new situations. She
and her co-workers found that babies who
showed the greater number of indications
of independence were less secure than
those who accepted care and direction. She
concluded from this that while all babies
show signs of both dependence and independence, the most secure baby is the one
who shows predominately more signs of dependence.

The items in Flint's scale deal with
bodily functions and center around feed-

ing, sleeping, elimination and reactions
to new situations. In essence, the test
consists of security items--those reflecting a state of dependence on adults and
those showing a desire for independence in
behaviors which the child is skillful
enough to do for himself. Insecurity items
are those reflecting behaviors that are
substitute devices.

Flint found the test to be reliable
and to differentiate between infants and
between poorly adjusted and well-adjusted
groups of infants.

DESIGN OF WALTERS'S STUDY

Of over ninety mothers and their
babies studied, fifty-eight had complete
data from which most of the results could
be analyzed. Subjects were selected on the
basis of the following criteria: prenatal
care--subjects showing any abnormality
during pregnancy or at birth were elimin-
ated; mothers' ages--between twenty-one
and thirty-two years; intact homes; non-
working mothers for the first year; non-
smoking mothers; middle-class socioeconomic background; white race. The majority of
births were first ones, and the socioeconomic status ranged from middle to upper-
middle class.

The method of measuring fetal activity devised by Walters (1964) was used,
with mothers recording the last two months
of pregnancy. During pregnancy the mothers
were given the Cattell Anxiety test (IPAT)
(Cattell 1963). Postnatally, they were
given the mother-infant interaction test
for overprotection (Schvaneveldt 1964) and

the Orthner adaptation of the Porter Parental Acceptance Scale and the Orthner
Authoritarian Scale (Orthner 1969).

Postnatally, the infants were tested
at three-month intervals on the Gesell
Developmental Schedules and for security
on the Flint Security Scale (Flint 1959).
At eighteen months, the infants were
placed in a nursery school with others
of the same age who were in the study. For
three months, they came twice weekly for
two hours. They re-entered the nursery
school when they were twenty-four months
of age and stayed until twenty-seven
months. At no time were there more than
eight children present, and the majority
of the time the number was closer to five
or six. Mothers were allowed in the nursery school. They sat at one of the room
and were available for the child to interact with if he wished.

At twenty-one and twenty-seven
months, the mother and the nursery school
teacher rated the child's behavior on
categories developed by Graham et al.
(1963). The instrument consisted of 209
items classified into thirteen categories,
with apprehension, inwardness, aggressiveness, hyperactivity,[1] demandingness, temperateness, emotionality, and inactivity
being among the categories. The teacher
also rated the children at twenty-one and
twenty-seven months on peer apprehension

---

1. Hyperactivity included twenty items.
The mean at twenty-one months for males
was 4.65; for females, 3.60. The mean at
twenty-seven months for males was 5.03;
for females 3.48. Therefore, the children
in the study presented were not to be construed as hyperactive.

and aggression.

Since the items on the scales de-
manded closer and more observations than
the nursery school teacher could make,
greater reliance was placed on the mother's ratings.

It should also be added that mothers
were very open in their discussions of
their children and were not threatened by
their children's behavior.

Correlations were determined between
fetal activity and the previously mentioned behaviors as well as interrelations
between behaviors. Data were analyzed for
each sex and for the total sample.

This chapter will focus on the part
maternal feelings, attitudes, and personality, as well as fetal activity, play
in the security of the infant.

PRENATAL

Greenacre (1941) in her classic paper
"The Predisposition to Anxiety" has raised
the question of the possibility of an anxiety reaction being potentially present in
intrauterine life and exhibited after
birth. She also asks the question whether
the fetus who cries in utero responds to
this discomfort by increased fetal activity. And what is the relation of this increased activity to anxiety? She comments:

In brief, then I would raise the
question of a preanxiety intrauterine
response to (threatening) stimuli,
consisting of reflex oral, muscular,
cardiac and possibly prerespiratory
reactions. This precedes the anxiety

pattern established by the birth
trauma, and probably augments it. It
is inconceivable to me that there
should be much psychic content to
this, and it may indeed be the stuff
of which blind, free floating, un-
analyzable anxiety is constituted--
sometimes adding just that overload
to the accumulation of postnatal
anxiety which produces the severe
neurotic (p. 74-75).

Greenacre also believes that although
the cortex may not function to any appre-
ciable degree in utero, it may be a passive recipient of anxiety, storing it for
future recall.

Sontag (1966) reported that pregnant
women undergoing extreme emotional stress
during pregnancy had babies with high
fetal activity, who when born were hyperactive, cried a great deal, and had gastrointestinal upsets in early infancy.
Walters (1965), in her study on the prediction of postnatal development from
fetal activity, had one infant of a highly
emotionally charged mother who fit Sontag's description; when the infant was
followed through for nine months postnatally, he had low Gesell developmental
scores, ranking in the lowest quartile at
three months and in the lower quartiles
through nine months.

An increase in fetal heartbeat and
fetal movements has been demonstrated when
the pregnant woman is subjected to increased noise or vibrations (Sontag 1966),
or when she is frightened (Liley 1965).
Thompson (1957) has shown that pregnant rats subjected to a stressful situation that produced a neurosis had off-

Anxiety

spring who exhibited neurotic behavior
at adolescence.

Since the nervous system of mother
and fetus are not connected anatomically,
the question is: How do maternal emotions
affect the fetus?

This has been explained by the fact
that extreme emotions of fear, hate,
anger, and so on, are accompanied by hormonal changes. Hormonal secretions of
mother and fetus unite to form a common
pool. Maternal hormones pass through the
placenta to the fetus and act upon the
nervous system of the fetus. The fetus
is stimulated to respond by an increase
in quick movements (Sontag 1944). It is
doubtful whether there is a psychological
affect associated with these movements,
but it is conceivable that a pattern of
irritability or reactivity to stimuli becomes established.

Nevertheless, we cannot discount entirely the psychic beginnings of intrauterine life. While cortical function is
either nonexistent or minimal, it appears
that subcortical areas associated with
emotional discharge are present by the
third month of gestation (Straub 1971).

Papez (1937) has said that emotion
implies not only a way of acting but a way
of feeling. The first is shown as "emotional expression" and the second as "emotional experience or subjective feeling."
He says emotional expression is dependent
upon the integrative action of the hypothalamus, while subjective emotional experience involves the participation of the
cortex.

The central emotive process of cortical origin may then be conceived

as being built up in the hippocampal formation and as being transferred to the mamillary body and
thence through the anterior thalamic
nuclei to the cortex of the gyrus
cinguli. The cortex of the cingular
gyrus may be looked on as the receptive region for the experiencing of
emotion as the result of impulses
coming from the hypothalamic region.
... Radiation of the emotive process
from the gyrus cinguli to other regions in the cerebral cortex would
add emotional coloring to psychic
processes (p. 19).

We predicted in this study that fetal
activity, considered as one measure of
constitutionality, would have a significant relation to apprehension and aggression when maternal factors were controlled. A one-tailed test was used in the
analysis of data.

Table 1 gives significant correlations of fetal activity with security, apprehension, and aggression (maternal influences not controlled). Only females
showed a correlation coefficient approach-
significance at $p < .05$ level for fetal
activity and apprehension. Fetal activity
has a negative relation with security at
three and twenty-four months for males;
that is, the higher the fetal activity the
lower the security. No such relationship
existed for females.

When maternal factors, logically believed and empirically shown, which could
contribute to constitutional aspects of
anxiety and aggression were partialled out
--that is, maternal anxiety, overprotection, acceptance, and three- and nine-

Table 1
Significant Correlations ($p < .05$) Between
Fetal Activity and Security or
Apprehension at 21 Months[1]

Males

3-mo. security	-.35 (37)[2]
24-mo. security	-.32 (37)

Females

Apprehension   .40 (21)[3]

---

1. Apprehension and aggression rated by mothers.
2. Numbers in parentheses indicate number in sample.
3. p approaching .05.

months security--a positive correlation was found between fetal activity and aggression in males at twenty-one months. A correlation approaching significance at the $p < .05$ level for apprehension and fetal activity and a nonsignificant correlation of .40 for aggression and fetal activity were shown for females (table 2). All other nonpartialled correlation coefficients between fetal activity and apprehension and aggression at twenty-one and twenty-seven months for males and between fetal activity and aggression for females were in the range .00 to .08 (nonsignificant). It should be mentioned that only apprehension and aggression were singled out for the above correlations with fetal activity.

It should be pointed out that when five factors were controlled and the two

Table 2
Correlations Between Fetal Activity and
Infant Apprehension and Aggression
at 21 Months[1]

Males

Aggression   .38 (37), $p < .05$.

Females

Aggression   .40 (21), n.s.
Apprehension   .46 (21), p approaching .05.

---

1. Maternal acceptance, anxiety, overprotection and 3- and 9-months security partialled out.

degrees of freedom accounted for, the number of degrees of freedom for the sample was increased to seven.

It would seem, therefore, that in this sample aggression has a constitutional correlate in fetal activity for males and one approaching significance for apprehension and fetal activity for females, with some suggestion of a possible correlate for aggression. Maternal factors of acceptance, overprotection, anxiety, and care that could affect infant security apparently, in this sample, were mitigating influences in apprehension and aggression.

As has been previously mentioned, Greenacre has made such a proposal regarding prenatal activity and anxiety, and Brody and Axelrad (1970), in summarizing research findings regarding prenatal responsiveness, have commented that fetal activity is never random but has pattern, direction, and effect. Winnicott (1965), in writing of fetal activity, believes motility is a forerunner of aggression and in earlier writings has made the point that originally aggressiveness is almost synonymous with activity. Honzik (1964) also views aggressiveness as possibly having a constitutional basis.

BIRTH

Greenacre (1941) believes research in the area of the birth process and its later effects on the child has been a neglected one. She believes that birth could very well organize the anxiety pattern combining the genetic or constitutional determinations with the uniqueness of the birth experiences of the infant.

McGrade et al. (1965) studied the newborn in regard to delivery difficulty. They found the length of labor to be significantly correlated with the number of previous births. Infants of longer labor were quiet when stimulated by having their foreheads rubbed. Shorter-labor infants tended to be more agitated when stimulated. McGrade's explanation was that this might be in accord with Greenacre's "sensory fatigue" or an adaptation to stimuli specific to labor.

Montagu (1965, 1971) has made the point that long labor involves contractions of the uterus that stimulate the skin. He says evidence supports the thesis that the uterine contractions of labor may be the beginning of caressing of the baby in the appropriate way (1971).

When short- and long-labor infants were compared (by the Mann-Whitney U test) on behavioral ratings by mothers at twenty-one months, significant differences were found in apprehension, hyperactivity, and in three- and twelve-month security (table 3). All differences were in favor of the long-labor infant; he was less apprehensive, less hyperactive, and more secure. No differences were found in six-months security. Mothers of long-labor infants had lower anxieties than did those of short-labor babies. All measures were statistically significant. It should be noted here that only the above-mentioned behavioral measures were compared. No difficult or abnormal pregnancies or births were used in the comparison. Tests were done to eliminate the possibility that birth order had any effect on the results.

These results are in line with Greenacre's and Montagu's theorizing concerning the birth process and longer labor.

POSTNATAL

Maternal acceptance for each sex was negatively correlated with authoritarianism (-.66 for males, and -.55 for females) at the $p < .01$ level. Maternal acceptance was negatively correlated with aggression at twenty-seven months (-.36) for males, and positively with temperateness at twenty-seven months (.47) for females. Both correlations were at the $p < .05$ level of significance.

Maternal overprotection for males positively correlated with aggression and with negativism at twenty-one months and

Table 3

Significance Differences in Behavioral Measures Between Long-Labor
(12 to 24 Hours) and Short-Labor (0 to 6 Hours) Infants
(Males and Females Combined)

Measure	Labor		U	Level of Significance
	Long (n=15) Median	Short (n=14)		
Apprehension at 21 mo.[1]	1.00	2.00	41.05	$p < .01$
Hyperactivity at 21 mo.[1]	4.50	6.00	53.50	$p < .025$
3-month security	0.44	0.39	31.50	$p < .001$
12-month security	0.42	0.38	49.00	$p < .01$
Maternal anxiety (IPAT)	25.50	30.00	50.00	$p < .01$

1. Rated by mothers.

negatively correlated with inactivity at twenty-seven months. For females, over-protection negatively correlated with peer apprehension at twenty-one months and with peer aggression at twenty-seven months (table 4). The sex differences found in the correlations may possibly be explained on constitutional bases interacting with environmental influences (see table 2).

Acceptance was measured by the mothers' responses as to how they would deal with behaviors of preschool children. Overprotection was tested by their responses to how they would deal with children's behavior in certain situations depicted in a film (Schvaneveldt 1964).

When maternal anxiety was correlated with infant security a negative relation-

Table 4
Significant Correlations ($p < .05$) Between
Overprotection and Behavioral
Measures of Infants

Males

Aggression at 21 mo.[1]	.36 (34)
Negativism at 21 mo.[1]	.35 (34)
Inactivity at 27 mo.[1]	-.44 (36)[2]

Females

Peer aggression at 27 mo.[3]	-.80 (13)[2]
Peer apprehension at 21 mo.[3]	-.61 (16)[4]

1. Rated by mother.
2. $p < .01$.
3. Rated by teacher.
4. p approaching .01.

ship was shown for males at three and nine months--that is, the more anxious the mother, the less secure the infant; and for females a negative relationship approaching significance at $p <$ .05 at 6 months (table 5).

In regard to overprotection, significant differences were found in maternal ratings, with mothers of girls receiving higher scores (8.35) than did mothers of boys (6.18) (t = 2.11, $p <$ .05).

The significant correlations between maternal anxiety and infant security are not too surprising in light of previous research studies (Newton 1963, Ottinger and Simmons 1964) and psychoanalytic thinking (Benedek 1949, Escalona 1952, A. Freud 1946). Anna Freud (1946) has written about the contagious emotional climate of the mother and Escalona (1952) of the proclivity of the baby to catch the anxiety of the mother.

Three-month security (table 6) in both sexes correlated negatively with peer apprehension at twenty-seven months--that

Table 5
Correlations Between Maternal Anxiety
(IPAT) and Infant Security

	Males	Females
Security at 3 mo.	-.50 (37)[1]	n.s.
Security at 6 mo.	n.s.	-.43 (19)[2]
Security at 9 mo.	-.40 (35)[3]	n.s.

1. $p <$ .01.
2. p approaching .05.
3. $p <$ .05.

Table 6

Significant Correlations ($p < .05$) Between Security and Apprehension and Between Security and Aggression

Security		Males	Females
at 3 mo.	Peer aggression at 21 mo.	.37 (26)[1]	.54 (16)
	Peer apprehension at 27 mo.	-.40 (28)	-.61 (13)
9 mo.	Peer aggression at 21 mo.	-.44 (22)	-.66 (15)[2]
	Peer apprehension at 27 mo.	-.40 (26)	-.51 (13)[1]
12 mo.	Aggression at 21 mo.[3]	-.35 (32)	n.s.
	Aggression at 27 mo.[3]	-.38 (34)	n.s.
	Peer aggression at 21 mo.[3]	n.s.	.54 (16)
18 mo.	Aggression at 27 mo.[3]	-.39 (36)	n.s.
	Peer aggression at 27 mo.	n.s.	-.55 (13)[1]
	Peer apprehension at 21 mo.[3]	n.s.	-.44 (16)[1]
24 mo.	Apprehension at 21 mo.[3]	n.s.	-.47 (20)
	Apprehension at 27 mo.[3]	-.50 (36)[2]	n.s.
	Aggression at 27 mo.[3]	n.s.	-.49 (19)[1]
	Peer apprehension at 21 mo.	n.s.	-.47 (16)[1]

1. p approaching .05.   2. $p < .01$.
3. Rated by mothers; other ratings made by teachers.

is, the more secure at three months, the less apprehensive at twenty-seven months, and positively with aggression at twenty-one months.

There were no significant correlations of security at six months with either apprehension or aggression. However, at nine, twelve, eighteen, and twenty-four months, security in males correlated negatively with either apprehension and/or aggression. At twelve months security in females correlated positively with peer aggression at twenty-one months, and at eighteen and twenty-four months it correlated negatively with either apprehension or aggression or both.

It would appear that, for the most part, security and apprehension and security and aggression were negatively correlated.

Vinson (1972), in her investigation of attachment behavior in black infant-mother pairs in the first year of life, found securely attached infants to be more secure, as measured by the Flint Security Scale, than insecurely attached babies. Nonattached infants were also significantly more secure than insecurely attached babies. There was no difference in security between securely attached and nonattached infants. Vinson's explanation was that nonattached babies may be late developers and classified as not-yet-attached infants (Ainsworth 1967, Bowlby 1969).

This explanation could very well be the right one, because the developmental quotients of the nonattached group in Vinson's study ranged from 96 to 120. Two babies had scores of 96 and only one a score of 120 (median of 100, mean of 104).

Table 7

Significant Correlations ($p < .05$) Between Security
and Behavioral Measures of Infants

Security		Males	Females
at 3 mo.	Security at 9 mo.	.54 (34)[1]	n.s.
	Emotionalness at 21 mo.	-.35 (33)	n.s.
	Temperateness at 21 mo.[4]	n.s.	.42 (17)[2]
	Temperateness at 27 mo.[4]	.42 (35)[3]	n.s.
	Hyperactivity at 27 mo.[4]	n.s.	.52 (13)[2]
	Inactivity at 21 mo.[4]	.41 (33)	n.s.
	Inactivity at 27 mo.[4]	n.s.	-.69 (13)[1]
	Demandedness at 21 mo.[4]	-.42 (30)	n.s.
	Negativism at 27 mo.[4]	n.s.	.64 (13)[3]
	Fetal activity	-.35 (37)	n.s.
at 6 mo.	Security at 9 mo.	.53 (34)[1]	n.s.
	Security at 12 mo.	.49 (36)[1]	.54 (19)[1]
	Security at 18 mo.	.59 (37)[1]	n.s.
	Security at 24 mo.	n.s.	.51 (18)
	Temperateness at 27 mo.[4]	.61 (35)[1]	n.s.
	Hyperactivity at 27 mo.[4]	n.s.	-.73 (12)[1]

Table 7 (continued)

Security		Males	Females
at 9 mo.	Security at 12 mo.	n.s.	.70 (12)[1]
	Security at 18 mo.	.50 (35)[1]	.49 (19)
	Security at 24 mo.[4]	.34 (34)	.43 (19)
	Emotionalness at 21 mo.[4]	n.s.	-.63 (16)[1]
	Inactivity at 21 mo.[4]	n.s.	-.55 (16)
	Independence at 21 mo.[4]	n.s.	.65 (16)[1]
	Temperateness at 27 mo.	.38 (33)	n.s.
at 12 mo.	Security at 18 mo.	.39 (36)	.52 (20)
	Security at 24 mo.	n.s.	.67 (20)[1]
	Emotionalness at 21 mo.[4]	n.s.	-.56 (17)
	Hyperactivity at 21 mo.	-.37 (32)	n.s.
	Hyperactivity at 27 mo.	-.34 (34)	n.s.
	Inwardness at 21 mo.	.38 (32)	n.s.
	Inwardness at 27 mo.[4]	n.s.	-.54 (13)[2]
	Temperateness at 27 mo.	.36 (34)	n.s.
at 18 mo.	Security at 24 mo.	.63 (37)[1]	.54 (20)[3]
	Emotionalness at 21 mo.	.45 (34)[3]	-.62 (17)[1,4]

Table 7 (continued)

Security		Males	Females
at 18 mo.	Temperateness at 27 mo.	.33 (36)	n.s.
	Demandedness at 27 mo.	n.s.	-.43 (19)[2]
	Compulsiveness at 27 mo.	.38 (36)	n.s.
	Inactivity at 27 mo.	n.s.	-.47 (19)
	Independence at 27 mo.	.35 (36)	n.s.
	Negativism at 27 mo.	n.s.	-.47 (19)
at 24 mo.	Hyperactivity at 27 mo.	-.35 (36)	-.56 (19)[3]
	Compulsiveness at 21 mo.	n.s.	-.57 (20)[1]
	Compulsiveness at 27 mo.	.40 (36)	n.s.
	Inactivity at 21 mo.	n.s.	-.59 (20)[1]
	Inwardness at 21 mo.	n.s.	-.46 (20)
	Independence at 27 mo.	.39 (36)	n.s.
	Temperateness at 27 mo.	n.s.	.61 (19)[1]
	Negativism at 27 mo.	n.s.	-.46 (19)

1. $p < .01$.   2. p approaching .05.   3. p approaching .01.
4. Rated by teachers; other ratings made by mothers.

Of the five infants in this group, four
were males. Means and medians of the two
other groups were 109, 107 and 109, 110.

Of the securely attached infants,
three were female and three male. It is
noteworthy that five females and two males
made up the insecurely attached group. It
is also interesting that the infants in
this group were so anxious and frightened
before separation from the mother that
they did not recover during the entire
strange situation, nor could they be
tested for object-permanence. Regarding
this, Vinson says, "In the case of these
infants, their high degree of insecurity paralyzed them in the object-permanence testing procedures and accentuat-
ed their retrieval efforts during person-
permanence testing" (p. 58). Gouin Décarie, T., et al. (1974), in reviewing
their studies and those of others, found
females, in comparison to males, showed
more negative reactions to strangers.

When infant security was correlated
with other behavioral measures (table 7),
the following points were noted. Security
ratings for males from three months on
correlated significantly with succeeding
ratings ($p < .01$). Security ratings for
females, beginning with six-months security, correlated significantly with succeeding ratings. Security in this sample appears to be a stable trait in both males
and females.

In view of the greater physiological
variability of the male infant, it is interesting that security at three months
would correlate with succeeding ratings.
However, Moss (1967), in a study of maternal and infant behavior at three weeks and
three months, found mothers of male babies

to differ significantly in time spent in
maternal contact, stressing musculature,
and stimulating/arousing the infant. When
infant behaviors were reported, it was
found that males spent significantly more
time fussing, crying and fussing, and ly-
ing supine. Therefore, not only did mothers spend more time with male babies in
activities that involved tactile, proprioceptive, and visual stimulation (see the
discussion on coenesthetic organization
in the introduction to this part), but
this was in response to the infant's
needs. That the state of the infant can
influence his behavior as well as the
mother's was recognized a long time ago by
Fries (1935). It is possible that this
could account for the earlier security
correlations with succeeding ones in
males.

    Other significant security correla-
tions of note for boys are the consistently positive ones with temperateness at
every rating with the exception of twenty-
four months, the positive ones at eighteen
and twenty-four months with independence
at twenty-seven months, and the negative
ones at twelve and twenty-four months with
hyperactivity at twenty-one and twenty-
seven months.

    For girls, security correlations of
note are the significant positive ones
with temperateness, the negative ones with
emotionality, demandedness, negativism,
and the twelve- and twenty-four months negative correlation with inwardness, which
is closely allied to apprehension.

    The only sex differences found be-
tween males and females in this study were
in hyperactivity at twenty-one months,
with boys being more active (t = 3.16,

p < .01), and inwardness at twenty-one
months, with girls being significantly
more inward (t = 2.58, p < .02). The inwardness scale included such items as
"acts nervous, worries a lot, gets sick to
stomach easily, bites his (or her) nails,"
and so on; these could be considered
"anxiety items."

SUMMARY

A review of the literature on security (Flint 1959) showed it to be rooted in
maternal responses to the needs of the infant and his acceptance of care. When this
happens, there is also an emotional tie
developed between mother and infant, and
the mutually satisfying interplay between
the two promotes a sense of self-worth,
trust, and a feeling of security in the
baby.

While self-demand feeding is important in the first several months, the infant soon develops his own pattern or
rhythm of eating, as he does with sleeping and other bodily functions. The infant
who has his needs met by a mother sensitive to them gradually learns to wait for
his food. When self-demand goes on too
long, it becomes a "permissive" care; and
insecurity is a product of a permissive
environment (Flint 1959).

Psychoanalysts have stressed the need
for contrast, as shown in the satisfac-
tion-frustration rhythmic experiences
(Mahler 1963). Frustration, when part of
this experience, is important in helping
to develop body boundaries that are pre-
cursors for a sense of identity (Jacob-

son 1964, Mahler 1963).

The results of the study on fetal activity (Walters 1966-71) presented here
showed that prenatal activity correlates
with aggression and approaches significance for apprehension at twenty-one
months when maternal variables are controlled. Females also showed correlations
approaching significance ($p < .05$) between
nonpartialled correlations of fetal activity and apprehension.

This, and the higher ratings of females on inwardness at twenty-one months
and the apparent anxiety items mentioned
earlier leads one to speculate that the
female is predisposed to anxiety.

The significant correlation between
fetal activity and aggression for males
when maternal variables were controlled
is interesting. While there were no differences in aggression ratings by mothers
between males and females, males showed
significant correlations between aggression and hyperactivity at twenty-one and
twenty-seven months. For females, the
correlation was shown only at twenty-
seven months. As mentioned earlier, males
and females differed significantly in
hyperactivity, with males having the
higher ratings. While males had higher
fetal activity scores than females, the
difference was not significant. It would
appear that perhaps the activity component
plays a significant role in the predisposition of the male toward aggressiveness.

When infants were divided into long-
and short-labor categories, significant
differences in apprehension and hyperactivity were shown at twenty-one months,
and in security at three and twelve
months. All differences were in favor of

the long-labor infant. Mothers of such infants were also less anxious.

Postnatally, infant security, overall, had negative correlations with apprehension and aggression--that is, the more
secure the infant, the less apprehensive
and aggressive he was at a later stage of
development. The secure infant also, for
the most part, had positive correlations
with temperateness and negative correlations with emotionality, demandedness,
hyperactivity, and inwardness.

3. PSYCHOPATHOLOGY OF INFANCY

Howard Protinsky

> Psychotic object relationships ...
> are restitution attempts of a rudi-
> mentary or fragmented ego, which
> serves the purpose of survival, as
> no organism can live in a vacuum and
> no human being can live in an object-
> less state.
>
> *Mahler (1960)*

Since the turn of the century when
Sigmund Freud made his important theoretical discoveries regarding childhood sexuality, researchers and theorists in the
field of human development have been concerned about experiential factors and the
development of psychopathology in the
child and adult. While much of the research has dealt with mother-child interaction, there is a growing body of work in
the field that has explored the role of
organic and fetal experiences in the etiology of psychopathology.

In this chapter, the author will look at important theoretical and empirical considerations specifically concerning the development of psychopathology in infancy. The role of organic factors will be examined as well as in utero experiences and mother-infant interaction.

PRENATAL AND CONSTITUTIONAL FACTORS

The mother-fetus interaction is an important variable in the understanding of the development of psychopathological symptoms in the human organism. Benedek (1956) suggests that the pregnant mother's feelings about herself and her newly conceived child influence the relationship long before the child is born. Anxiety-provoking conditions, especially in the first trimester of pregnancy, may act to change the internal physiological and biochemical conditions to such an extent that the fetus is damaged. In his research at the Fels Institute, Sontag (1944) discovered that the mother's emotional state can have a lasting influence on the organism. If the mother is involved in a stressful situation, the motility of the fetus may be influenced toward hyperactivity in utero. Mothers who are under stress tend to produce babies who are hyperactive, irritable, and often have gastrointestinal disturbances. For Sontag, these infants are already neurotic at birth.

Greenacre (1941) hypothesizes that anxiety reactions exist in the fetus prior to birth and that these may leave an "organic stamp" on the fetus that predisposes

him to anxiety after birth. She maintains
that traumatic stimuli such as loud
noises, strong vibrations, umbilical cord
entanglements, and other unknown intrauterine stressful stimuli cause reflexive
oral, muscular, and cardiac reactions that
are a beginning form of anxiety. These
responses are organized into an anxiety
pattern during the birth trauma, with the
infants tending to be anxious after birth.
This organic stamp retards their developing recognition of the environment as
separate from self and leads to an increased narcissism that forms the core of
later pathological difficulties.

In pointing to the birth trauma as an
important aspect in anxiety formation,
Greenacre has the support of Otto Rank
(1929). Rank theorized that the trauma experienced at birth predisposes every individual for later anxiety. The greater
the trauma, the more the infant will experience anxiety. On the research level,
Wile and Davis (1941) indicated that
children delivered with forceps--which is
a type of trauma--show a general reduction
of energy in addition to increased irritability and anxiety.

In looking toward constitutional aspects of the fetus and infant that predispose him to psychopathology independent
of the mother's interaction, Ornitz (1969)
reviewed a number of studies of a psycho-
physiological and neurophysiological nature. He arrived at the conclusion that
there is a basic perceptual disorder in
infants who suffer from severe psychopathology. The infant experiences either
a heightened sensory perception, a flood-
ing of sensory data so that discrimination
and significance are lost, or he may be

entirely cut off from sensory experience.
These dysfunctions produce either hyperactivity or withdrawal. Mahler (1962),
Goldfarb (1961), and Fish et al. (1965)
all agree that in many schizophrenic infants there seems to be an underlying
organic problem that yields perceptual and
cognitive difficulties.

The studies of Weil and of Thomas
et al. (1970) have given much support to
the notion that there are inborn differences in infants that can result in psychopathological behavior upon interacting
with the environment. Weil has postulated
a "basic core" that is a fundamental layer
in the psychic structure; due to experiential factors, the core emerges the first
few weeks after birth. At one end are the
infants who are potentially sturdy and
adapt easily, and at the other end are
those who have a brittle makeup and are
hypersensitive and anxious. The degree to
which these two basic cores manifest themselves depends to a great extent upon the
mother-infant interaction. A warm, suppor-
tive mother may do much to ease the innate
psychopathological symptoms of anxiety in
the hypersensitive infant.

Thomas et al. have asserted that a
basic component of the child's constitutional individuality is his temperament,
of which there are nine categories: activity level, rhythmicity (regularity), approach or withdrawal, adaptability, threshold of responsiveness, intensity of reaction, quality of mood, distractibility,
and attention span. These components may
combine to produce one of three temperamental patterns: the difficult child, the
easy child, and the slow to warm up child.
The difficult child is seen as having the

psychopathological symptoms of irregular
sleep and feeding, slow acceptance of new
experiences, frequent periods of loud
crying, and violent temper tantrums. However, it is important to realize that it
is not the distinct individual temperament
alone that produces maladaptive behavior
but the innate characteristics in relation
to the environment. The nurturing mother
who is tuned in to her difficult child's
individuality may be able to move him
toward more adaptive behavior, while the
non-nurturing mother may produce more
pathological behavior in her infant.

Thus, prenatal and consititutional
elements can play a major role in the etiology of psychopathology in the infants.
They also are important in terms of personality adjustment in later life. However, it seems evident that the major concern should not be with the organic factor
in isolation but with the organic factor
in its interaction with the environment.

MOTHER-CHILD INTERACTION

The establishment of object relations
is a crucial task for the newborn in order
to achieve psychological health. The infant must move from an undifferentiated
state to one of perceiving himself as separate from his environment (for a discussion of this aspect of development see
chapter 1).

Winnicott has warned that when there
is poor maternal care, severe ego impairment may take place at best or annihilation of the ego at worst. In agreeing with
Winnicott, Mahler (1952) maintains that it

is precisely at the time of separation-individuation that severe emotional disturbance may take place. Infantile autism may result if the child is unable to perceive the mother emotionally as a representative of the outside world. Childhood psychosis may result if the infant's mental representation of mother remains fused with the self. These infants maintain the symbiotic relationship and never experience separation. Des Lauriers (1967) agrees that childhood psychosis seems to be a lack of awareness of bodily boundaries and a lack of experiencing oneself as a separated and differentiated individual capable of establishing a stable relationship with a mother figure. If the schizophrenic child could invest enough attention and interest in himself as a separate organism, he could then experience his own needs and seek their fulfillment. Melanie Klein (1964), one of the foremost child analysts, sees object relations as being extremely important in the formation of psychopathology in infancy. Childhood depression is seen as a result of movement from a part object relation to a whole object relation--that is, the object relation moves from part of the mother, such as her breast, to mother herself. With the lack of a consistent and warm relationship with the mother at this time, the infant develops extreme anxiety concerning the loss of the loved object (the mother). For Klein, anxiety over the loss of mother is the most painful affect in human development.

In addition to the necessity of a warm, nurturing, consistent relationship with a mothering figure for the formation of adequte object relations, Erik Erikson

(1959) has pointed out that these factors are necessary for the establishment of a sense of basic trust in the infant. Trust, in his view, is the "cornerstone of a healthy personality," and he points to the necessity of mutuality between infant and mother. This includes the consistent meeting of the infant's needs by the mother and the infant's response to the mother's ministrations. If trust and mutuality are not established, the infant learns to mistrust both self and environment. This can lead to such personality traits as not being able to depend or rely upon other persons or self, feelings of pessimism and despair, and feelings of abandonment. In its worst form, childhood psychosis could result.

Central to Erikson's theory of trust establishment is the consistent maternal object. With multiple mothering, one might find some degree of personality disorder, depending upon the type of mothering experience. Rabin (1958) and Bettelheim (1969) lend empirical support to this proposition by reporting that kibbutz-raised children tend to lack emotional depth in their interpersonal relationships. These children are able to maintain satisfactory relationships; but all relationships tend to be on the same level. Ainsworth (1963), in her study of mother-infant interaction among the Ganda, suggested that human infants are predisposed toward one person. Her experience is that even in cultures in which multiple mothering is used, equal division of mothering functions is not likely. Thus the infant develops a first attachment to the mother figure who takes over the major child care functions. Margaret Mead

(1962), however, has disagreed. She states that the conviction that the primary child care functions must be taken over by one figure if the child is to develop adequately is a culture-bound assumption. She believes that children who grow up in cultures in which there are many good mother figures learn to trust more people and are therefore better able to tolerate separation from the mother. She also feels that these infants develop more complex personalities due to more identifications. Although the evidence concerning the controversy over multiple mothering is far from conclusive, most authorities do agree that a nurturing mothering experience is needed for sound emotional health.

Infant feeding has long been an area studied in relation to personality development. Most of the studies relating oral gratification to psychopathology and personality development have operated from a psychoanalytical base. Freud (1905) has stressed that the need for food involves a need to suck and that gratification or frustration of this oral drive will affect the personality of the developing infant. Lack of oral gratification is said to lead to anxiety, insecurity, the need for constant reassurance, and impatience. Maximum gratification is assumed to occur with breast feeding that is regulated by the child's hunger rather than the clock, and gradual weaning that is delayed until the infant is ready. Heinstein (1963), however, conducted a comprehensive study that revealed no relationship between psychological adjustment and breast or bottle feeding. Caldwell (1964a), in a review of the literature on breast versus bottle feeding, concluded that no clear adjustment patterns have been demonstrated as a consequence of the type of feeding. Sears et al. (1957) demonstrated that children who were weaned very severely showed more upset during weaning. Murphy (1962) found that oral gratification during the first six months tends to leave the baby tension free, to facilitate good differentiation, and to foster good self-concept, while Goldman-Eisler (1953) demonstrated that children weaned early tended to demonstrate signs of oral pessimism in their personalities.

David Levy (1928) conducted a classical study in the early part of this century that supports the hypothesis that failure to satiate the oral drive with nutritive sucking will lead to compensatory non-nutritive mouthing or sucking—namely, thumb-sucking. In other studies, Simsarian (1947) and Sears and Wise (1950) have suggested that the oral drive is strengthened, not satiated, by the continued nutritive sucking, and that it is the strength of the oral drive and not the frustration that leads to thumb-sucking and oral pessimism. Although the controversy still continues, Yarrow (1954) attempted a solution by suggesting that during early infancy frustration may lead to fixation and non-nutritive sucking, while prolonged satisfaction of the drive may lead to overgratification and fixation.

Another important variable in the development of psychopathology of the infant is the degree of parental pathology present. Parents with deviant personalities are apt to effect faulty family patterns and nurturant dysfunctions. Studies by Garner and Wenar (1959) showed data concerning maternal attitudes and behavior in

relation to infant pathology. Findings
were that mothers of psychosomatically ill
children and seriously ill children basi-
cally found early infant care unrewarding
and had fewer positive attitudes toward
their infants; thus the infants experienced a deficiency in mothering. Spitz
(1965) has reported research that gives
weight to the hypothesis that, since the
mother is the dominant active partner in
the dyad of mother and child, disorders
of her personality will be reflected in
disorders of the child. Spitz uses the
term "psychotoxic" disturbances to describe improper mother-child relations and
maintains that in addition to the qualitatively disturbed relationship there may
also be some congenital elements operat-
ing. The conjunction of these two elements
leads to psychopathology.

Spitz (1965) has listed six different
conditions, each of which is related to a
particular maternal behavior pattern. The
first of these diseases is coma in the
newborn, which is accompanied by vomiting,
extreme pallor, and reduced sensitivity.
Spitz relates this condition to primary
overt rejection by the mother, who may
even refuse to nurse her child. The rejection may not be against the child as an
individual but against the fact of having
a child. Children who are treated this
way have to be taught how to suck by repeated stimulation of their oral zone.

The three-month colic is the second
disease described by Spitz. After the
third week of life and continuing into the
third month, the infant screams in the
afternoon. Feeding may calm him only tem-
porarily, and the pains may last for several hours. After reviewing the work of

several researchers, Spitz concludes that
there are two factors responsible for this
condition: congenital hypertonicity and
primary anxious overconcern on the part
of the mother. As if to compensate for her
unconscious hostility toward the child,
the mother feeds the child at every sign
of distress. Her feeding thus increases
the infant's excessive intestinal activity
even more. This disorder self-terminates
around the third month of life because the
infant can now rid himself of tension
through active movements of the body.

Infantile eczema is a third condition. It appears in the second half of the
first year and disappears between the
twelfth and fifteenth month. Congenital
predisposition in the form of increased
cutaneous excitability and an attitude of
anxiety about their children in mothers
were the two factors found to be associated with its incidence. The maternal anxiety seemed to conceal unusually large
amounts of unconscious repressed hostility. Spitz surmises that permanent traces
are left on the later personality development of these children. As the eczematous
infant acquires locomotion after the first
year of life and is then able to seek contact and satisfaction with other persons
and things, the symptom is removed.

Spitz's fourth description concerns
infants whose principal activity is violent rocking. These infants are exposed to
marked oscillation between pampering and
hostility from their mothers. The mothers
tend to be infantile personalities with a
lack of control over their aggression. The
babies are exposed to outbursts of fond-
ling and outbursts of rage and hostility.
The mother's inconsistent behavior retards

object relations, and thus the libidinal drive is discharged narcissistically in the form of rocking.

Fecal play, the fifth syndrome, is found to be associated with depression among mothers. These mothers show inter- mittent mood swings, varying from extreme hostility with rejection to extreme over- solicitousness. Psychoanalytically, this is explained by the notion that as the mother withdraws into her depression, the child experiences the object loss. He therefore replaces mother with another ob- ject, feces, which is readily available.

The last of the psychotoxic diseases is hyperthymia. This is a syndrome charac- terized by the child's proficiency with inanimate objects but with a conspicuous social retardation and hostility when ap- proached. Mothers of these children are found generally in intellectual circles and have a conscious conflict in their feelings toward the child. The infant is not loved for itself but serves as a satisfactory outlet for narcissistic and exhibitionistic impulses. The mother feels guilt concerning this and compensates with syrupy sweetness. The fathers tend to be aggressive, loud, and exhibitionistic in relation to their children and may fre- quently frighten them by rough handling.

In contrast to the psychotoxic dis- eases are the conditions of anaclitic de- pression and hospitalism that are the con- sequence of a quantitative deficiency of mothering (Spitz 1965). In studying in- fants who had a good, warm relationship with their mothers in the first six months of life but who suffered partial emotional deprivation in the second six months, Spitz described a set of symptoms known as

"anaclitic depression." Children who were
separated from their mothers for one to
three months developed symptoms of clinging, weeping, weight loss, facial rigidity, and motor retardation, as well as developmental quotient decreases. If the
mother was returned to the infant during
this time, the infant was able to achieve
a recovery, although in many cases it was
only partial. If separation from the mother persists after five months, the symptoms are irreversible, and death may result in some cases. These results were obtained only if no adequate mother substitute was provided.

Although studies in the area of maternal separation and maternal deprivation
have not been conclusive, results of classical research by Bowlby (1960) and Goldfarb (1943b) have indicated that problems
in the quantitative aspect of mother-infant relationship may produce deviations
in the psychology of the infant. The child
may develop an inadequate ego and a defec-
tive superego. In addition, some children
may become socially apathetic and be very
withdrawn while others may manifest the
syndrome of "affect hunger," which is
characterized by continuous demands for
attention and affection. Because of the
complexity of the variables involved, however, the area of maternal deprivation and
separation is still one that needs a great
deal more research.

SUMMARY

Certainly the research and theoretical attempt to discover the etiology of

childhood psychopathology is still in its
infancy and far from conclusive. Although
specific etiological factors are difficult
to delineate, all of the research explored
in this chapter, including that dealing
with organic factors, has pointed to the
need of every infant for quality maternal
care. Without it, ego development is pre-
carious at best. The problem, however, is
deciding what makes up the complex variable of quality maternal care. More
research needs to be directed toward this
area.

PART II

SOCIAL DEVELOPMENT

This section is concerned with the mother-infant interaction that influences the social development of the infant. Dr. Crum discusses social learning and reinforcement history in infancy, with implications for the disadvantaged. He also brings to the reader suggestions of a systematic analysis of behaviors and examples of specific behaviors for providing positive and optimal social learning experiences. Dr. Walters and Mrs. Wilhoit discuss the ontogenesis of socialization, the importance of the infant as a "socializer," and the factors influencing the development of object relations. Mr. Stumpff discusses infant day care from the standpoint of whether it can adequately meet the needs of the infant in the emotional, social and perceptual-cognitive domains.

INTRODUCTION TO PART II

C. Etta Walters

Of men and women he makes fathers and
mothers.

Rheingold (1968)

The human infant at birth is a social
being (Rheingold 1971). The helplessness
of the neonate necessitates contact with
other human beings for survival; his rep-
etoire of sensibilities and capabilities
enable him to signal his needs and to react to people and other stimuli in his environment. Rheingold thus sees the infant,
as not only actively involved in social
interaction but as a prime instigator of
it. In fact, she says, "He socializes
others more than he is socialized"
(p. 779).
The mutual interaction of infant and
mother results in a modification of behaviors for both. However, we are more accustomed to thinking of mother-infant interaction as a one-way street, with mother
and/or father influencing the child's behavior. Rheingold lists some means by

which the baby changes parental actions. They are:

1. The cry tells the mother he is in need of something. Because of its aversiveness, the parent acts to stop it.

2. The smile, because it is rewarding, makes mother's care worthwhile.

3. The infant's vocalizations, more often than not, promote parental vocalizations.

4. The pleasure felt in taking care of the young infant is, in itself, a rewarding experience.

5. The signals the baby gives his caretakers tell them of his special preferences and modifies their behavior to react to his needs.

6. The helplessness of the infant evokes feelings of compassion and tenderness in the caretaker and gives him a feeling of usefulness in the world.

Escalona (1973) and her co-workers have observed and catalogued the behaviors of two infants a minimum of two hours weekly from birth to the end of the child's second birthday. Behavior was recorded in terms of infant behavior rather than in terms of what his "social partner did or intended to do" (p. 206). It was also categorized as social input (infant's response to another human being) and social output (infant's social initiations to another individual and his response to that person in a "forward and sustained manner").

The two infants studied were both firstborn and raised in their own homes, and both were on the lower end of the "below average" group on Warner's scale of social status. However, the two homes were entirely different in educational level, ethnic background, values, interests, childrearing practices, and other factors.

The interesting and important facts emerging from these observations were as follows:

1. Social inputs and outputs in the two infants were amazingly regular and similar. In one infant there were 200 contacts per 300 minutes of "waking time" at 3 months (64 percent); for the same infant the rate was around 95 percent at 6 months.

2. Social input and social output curves were similar.

3. There was a sharp increase in social inputs from birth on to 7 or 8 months of age, which was followed by irregularities, not appreciably affecting the baseline, until 12.3 months.

4. The number of social inputs decreased between 12.3 and 15.0 months, which was coincidental to an increase in locomotion.

5. At 16.4 months and through the 22nd month there was a definite but slow increase in social inputs.

6. Both infants had more social inputs between 20.6 and 21.9 months.

7. Social inputs for the entire age range could be categorized into 17 kinds of modalities, with nonspecific ones being most frequent.

8. Thirteen new and "more differentiated" social output modalities were evidenced with age.

9. After 5 months, initiatory inputs were greater than reactive ones in the social inputs category, with the ratio between the two stabilizing after 13 1/2 months.

10. Analysis of the percent of initiatory social inputs and percent of reactive social outputs showed the more the infant, after 8 months or so, was subjected to initiatory social inputs by others, his behavior became less initiatory and more reactive. Regarding this point Escalona says:

> It is quite possible that during the second year of life a large amount of socially mediated stimulation that is not directly connected with the child's behavior at the moment serves to decrease spontaneous, self-directed behavior on the child's part, at least in the social realm. The hypothesis has obvious implications for the planning of enrichment or compensatory programs for young children (p. 222).

11. The frequency of certain social inputs reactive to the frequency of related social outputs led Escalona to comment, "For instance, the more a baby is

shown things and given information the
more will he himself show things and offer
information to others" (p. 225).

12. Compliance to requests of others
was not related to compliance of others to
the child's requests; nor were demands
made or restraints exercised in proportion
to the degree to which demands were suc-
cessful or the degree to which the child
offered resistance. Therefore it was concluded that while reinforcement learning
theory could possibly account for some
"specific patternings of behavior"
(p. 227), it could not account for many
others.

Escalona remarks that the regulari-
ties observed would not be so impressive
if the two infants had been exposed to
similar experiences. The differences are
attested to by the fact that at two years
of age the two children were "totally different and distinct little personalities"
(p. 232). Escalona urges that similar observations be conducted on larger groups
of children.

The results of a study by Stayton et
al. (1971) on infant obedience and maternal behavior have relevance for socialization and learning theory. Twenty-five
white, middle-class infants, ages nine to
twelve months, were studied in their homes
for four hours at three-week intervals
during the first year of life. The researchers observed "compliance to commands," which they defined as "the percentage of instances in which the baby
complied with his mother's verbal commands" (p. 1062). They also checked for
internalized control, that is, "self-in-

hibiting, self-controlling behavior" (p.
1062). Maternal variables were sensitivity, acceptance, cooperation, and their
counterparts. The frequency of verbal commands was also recorded, as was "frequency
of physical intervention." "Floor freedom"
was also noted; this referred to the extent the infant was allowed to be free on
the floor or in a walker while awake.

The researchers found that obedience,
or "compliance to commands," was correlated with the sensitivity of maternal response to infant cues and not to the frequency of the mother's command or her
physical interventions:

> The findings suggest that a disposi-
> tion toward obedience emerges in a
> responsive, accommodating social en-
> vironment without extensive training,
> discipline, or other massive attempts
> to shape the infant's course of de-
> velopment. These findings cannot be
> predicted from models of socializa-
> tion which assume that special inter-
> vention is necessary to modify the
> otherwise social tendencies of chil-
> dren (pp. 1065-66).

They explain the results in terms of an
ethological-evolutionary model of social
development.

In light of Escalona's (1973) results
regarding compliance to requests and those
of Stayton et al. (1971), it would seem as
though the traditional response-reinforce-
ment principle should be re-evaluated and
possibly replaced. Estes (1972) sees the
principles of reinforcement in terms of
informational-feedback theory, and not
just in terms of the "obsolescent view" of

reward and punishment. Reinforcement, he
says, must consider information that the
individual has which enhances or decreases
the possibility of the anticipated reward.
Bindra (1974) proposes that a child learns
to perform certain acts not by the traditional response reinforcement principle
but by following and observing the mother;
that is, the stimulus contingencies of
various objects in the environment and the
mother's actions and reactions to these
objects. Thus while the child's actions
may not be the same as those of the mother, they would tend to be similar to them,
especially if the child's motivational
state is the same as that of the mother at
the time of observation. Bindra says, "In
other words, the critical requirement is
not that the learner observe the model being reinforced but only that he observe
the model's prereinforcement transactions
with certain discriminative stimuli" (p.
2]0).

Only too often the effects of day
care have been evaluated as to cognition
with a neglect of the socioemotional affects. The critical issues regarding socioemotional affects seem to hinge on the
age of entrance into day care, which involves separation from the mother; the
quality of the mother-infant attachment
relationship; and the competency and sensitivity of the day-care personnel, who
are the mother substitutes.

Very few researchers have examined
the long-term results of day care, with
Caldwell et al. (1970) being an exception.
Even though the latter researchers found
no adverse effects after a period of approximately fourteen to eighteen months
(see chapter 6 for details), they did find

day-care children to be more dependent on other persons in their environment than were the controls. Although Caldwell attributed this to their greater breadth of attachment, Bowlby pointed out to her that it could possibly be due to overanxious attachments caused by frequent separations (Ainsworth 1973). For this reason, Ainsworth says she advocates qualitative determinations of attachment relationsips rather than strength of attachment behaviors.

Anna Freud in many of her writings has said that all separation can be viewed as maternal rejections, no matter what the cause. If this is true, it appears that we should evaluate the factors that reduce the stress associated with separation.

The results of some well-controlled studies by Moore (1964, 1969) showed that children who entered a "stable" day-care environment before twenty-four months of age were somewhat insecure; those experiencing "unstable" day care showed definite signs of insecurity.

Blehar (1973) found day-care and home-care children to differ in the quality of their relationships with their mothers when seen in an unfamiliar environment. Those who entered day care at age three were significantly more distressed than were home-reared children upon reunion with their mothers. Those entering day care at age two showed behavior typical of detachment exhibited after major separations. The day-care centers were those of a traditional nursery school, and the children from both groups came from "stable, middle class homes."

The following points regarding day care have been culled from the sources noted and appear to the editor to summarize the critical issues.

1. The caretaker of young children should be one who is of "emotional importance" to the child (Escalona 1967).

2. "Interaction with a mother figure, with resulting attachment is essential for healthy development" (Ainsworth]967, p. 77).

3. Variability in competency of the mother during the critical period of three to four weeks may be an important precursor of later anxiety (Benjamin 1963).

4. During the preobject stage a substitute mother may suffice if she is sensitive in recognizing and meeting the needs of the infant (Benjamin 1963).

5. Constancy of the individual who takes care of the infant is important, as it is she who comes to know the infant and responds to his needs and particular personality (Escalona 1967).

6. "A stimulating, person-animated environment" is necessary, as one cannot provide a rich stimulating environment designed to enhance cognitive development without the human factor, that is, one who reacts individually to a child who is interacting with inanimate objects (Escalona 1967).

7. Full-time group day care may have adverse effects on youngsters under age four (Ainsworth 1973).

8. Children three years and over usually can adjust to half-day nursery schools if they are not already insecure in their attachment relationships (Ainsworth 1973).

9. Factors which tend to promote stress in any separation are: unfamiliar environments, inadequate substitute caretakers, many caretakers, unfamiliar foods and routines, demands and disciplines which are out of the ordinary, and bodily restrictions (Robertson and Robertson 1971).

10. In addition, factors reducing stress--that is, those opposite to ones provoking it--are responses to toilet demands should be the same as the child is used to, and he should have some familiar possession with him (Robertson and Robertson 1971).

11. The psychological status of the child should be considered. This includes attention to the following topics (listed by Robertson and Robertson):

Ego maturity. The child should have reached the level of ego development where he can tolerate quantities of unpleasure without resorting to defense mechanisms.

Object constancy. The child who can maintain a positive image of the mother regardless of frustration has reached the level of object constancy. When this has occurred separations can be longer, dependent upon the strength of this constancy. In regard to this Anna Freud says, "Thus, even if it remains impossible to name the chronological age when separations can be tolerated, according to the

developmental line it can be stated when
they become phase-adequate and nontrauma-
tic, a point of practical importance for
the purposes of holiday for the parents
. . ., entry into nursery school, etc."
(A. Freud 1963, p. 249).

*Quality of mother-infant relation-
ship.* As noted above, the securely attached child can tolerate separations better than the insecurely attached one.

Defense organization. A. Freud (1963)
says the ego wins when its defense mechanisms are able to confine the development
of anxiety and displeasure, thereby modifying the instincts, so that some sort of
gratification is obtained . . . "thereby
establishing the most harmonious relations
possible between the id, the superego, and
the forces of the outside world" (p. 176).

Preparation for separation. The mother who takes the child to day care and
spends some time there with him, who talks
about the fun of going to the center before the event, and who encourages the
child to talk about his experiences while
there is helping to allay any separation
anxiety. If the child revolts against going and staying there, or if he appears to
have adjusted to the experience by a de-
nial of the mother's love upon reunion
with her, and if these persist, the infant
or child should not be forced to go to day
care. If it is necessary that he be given
care, the first choice would be for a
caretaker to come into the home and care
for him; or for him to stay with a friend-
ly and sensitive mother figure in her
home.

4. SOCIAL LEARNING AND

REINFORCEMENT HISTORY:

IMPLICATIONS FOR THE DISADVANTAGED

Joseph E. Crum

Rings and other jewels are not gifts
but apologies for gifts.
The only gift is a portion of
thyself.

Ralph Waldo Emerson

According to Hunt (1961), the importance of preverbal experience as contrib-
uting to later personality development
originated with Freud (1905) and his theory of psychosexual development. Much earlier, however, Rousseau (1792) discussed
the preverbal period as an opportune time
to toughen a child by early exposure to
pain and cold.

Erikson's (1963) popular neopsychoan-
alytic theory, and specifically his initial stage of development, attributes the in-

dividual's basic tendency toward later op-
timism or pessimism as almost totally determined during the preverbal period. He
posits that a firm sense of personal
trustworthiness forms the basis for identity, for being oneself, and for being
all right--or in contemporary transactional terms, being OK (Harris 1969).

In terms of intellectual development,
it was not until the 1940s that preverbal
experience was recognized as influencing
development in this domain. Hebb (1949),
concerned with the physiological correlates of intellectual behavior, stated
that the intrinsic regions of the cerebrum
must be properly programmed by preverbal
experience if the mammalian organism is
later to function effectively as a problem
solver.

The importance of early experiences
and their affects upon later development
and functioning have resulted not only
from theoretical formulations but from re-
search-orientated positions as well; Hess
and Shipman (1965), White and Castle
(1964), White and Held (1966), Denenberg
(1964, 1967), Fowler (1964), Bowlby
(1960), Harlow (1958), and Spitz (1950)
are only a few of those who have conducted
research in this area.

The main body of this research is
compatible with Fowler's (1964) position
that more rapid and higher levels of
learning take place during the infant's
most rapid and early growth period, which,
according to Aldrich (1946), Dekaban
(1959), and others, occurs during the
first year of life. It is during the first
six months of postnatal life that the
brain doubles its birth weight; by the end
of the first year, it triples that weight.

The rapid change taking place in neonatal and infant brain cells logically follows Hebb's (1949) concept of cell assemblies and phase sequences. According to Hebb, the cell assembly is a brain process that corresponds to a particular sensory event or a common aspect of a number of sensory events. For Hebb, the importance of early environmental experience is heavily stressed; based on exposures, cell assemblies are built up as a result of stimulating conditions. The phase sequence is a series of assembly activities, temporally integrated, resulting in one current in the stream of "thought" or memory.

Hebb's "thinking model" describes the infant as an active and participating organism; his theory is reasonably compatible with Piaget's (1952) preoperational stage of assimilation and accommodation as well as Bruner's (1964) period of enactive representation. It also seems that all early experience, regardless of sensory modality, can be integrated into Hebb's conceptual framework. In this connection, the actual behaviors involved in developing a sense of trust can be comprehended as composed of cell assemblies and phase sequences.

Hebb's concepts have been selected as a point of departure for this chapter because of their basic simplicity and adaptability to social behavior, and because it is felt that none of the material dealing with development, whether cognitively or language orientated, is irrelevant to social learning. But at this point in time, they preclude empirical validation. The purpose of this chapter will be to integrate testable concepts, couched in social learning theory, into Erikson's ini-

tial stage of human development. Bijou and
Baer's (1961, 1965) empirical theory of
child development and current research in
social learning during the first few
months of life will serve as the main
source of integrating material. In fact,
social learning and early social reinforcement history will occupy a central
position in this chapter, with implications for later development in disadvantaged children sharing major considera-
ation.

Justification for Erikson's (1963)
neoanalytic theory is threefold: (1) As
stated above, Erikson's formulations place
considerable importance on preverbal experience, and the resolution of each stage
or "epigenetic crisis" is essential for
continuing development. (2) Erikson's major variables are social forces as they
operate on the human organism at different
stages of biological and physical maturity
and are closely related to social learning
theory (Reese and Lipsitt 1970). (3)
Erikson's personality components arise
from sociocultural demands, thus affording
implications for the disadvantaged (Beiser
1965). Bijou and Baer (1961), in their empirical theory of child development, describe basic behaviors appearing to relate
to Erikson's trust stage. In addition, Bijou and Baer clearly define reinforcement
history as those historical variables influencing current behavior or the effect
of past interactions on present interactions. They view behaviors as a function
of events in the present situation and
based on previous interactions.

Bijou and Baer (1965) see the mother
as an important stimulus for her infant
and describe stimulus components of the

mother that are of special significance
for the future development of her infant.
The greatest number of reinforcement techniques are performed by the mother in
close physical relationship to the infant.
In other words, when a mother is close to
her infant, reinforcement follows--or, for
non- or anti-behaviorists, "good things
happen" and this usually occurs after a
short delay; when the mother is not so
close, reinforcement follows but only
after a longer delay , or possibly not at
all. An important consideration relating
to proximity is that under certain cir-
cumstances its function may become totally
reversed, that is, from a positive to negative reinforcer.

Paying attention to the baby can certainly be considered a component of trust.
Like proximity, attention includes a variety of stimuli that rapidly become social
reinforcers. Actual physical components of
attention include looking at, turning to,
facial changes, and cessation of other activity. Another critical characteristic of
mother's attending behavior concerns her
giving attention to "bad" behavior more
often and more consistently than to "good"
behavior.

A third and final stimulus component
is affection toward the infant. Included in
this category are such acts as smiling,
kissing, hugging and patting, special
crooning tones of voice, nuzzling, hair
ruffling, tickling, and so on. Each mother's style of nurturance will be that
which will be maximally reinforcing for
her child at a later date (Bijou and Baer
1965).

Studies reviewed by Schaffer and
Emerson (1964) indicate that by the age of

four weeks infants react to social stimulation by reducing bodily activity
(Shirley 1933); the first smile is evidenced at six weeks (Buhler 1930); from
two months and beyond the infant can recognize the mother (Griffiths 1954); and by
the first quarter-year period, the infant
may vocalize in response to another's
speech (Gesell and Amatruda 1947). It
seems, however, in agreement with Schaffer
and Emerson, that the descriptive milestones described above contribute little
to understanding environmental variables
responsible for reaching certain stages.
Important information is needed about the
mechanisms controlling the appearance of
the developmental milestones.

The studies of Wolff (1963), Brackbill (1958), Rheingold, et al. (1959),
Etzel and Gewirtz (1967), Weisberg (1963),
Rubenstein (1967), Wahler (1967), and
others show that the young infant is
highly sensitive to environmental variables in the form of social reinforcers
and that social reinforcement is effective
in strengthening and maintaining a number of responses. In fact, operant conditioning and social learning research
have demonstrated that the human infant
from the first days of his life is an active and adaptive organism as well as an
organism able to react reflexively.

Couched in social learning theory,
the following studies exemplify areas of
research attempting to delineate variables influencing the acquisition of certain behaviors. Since it is beyond the
scope of this chapter to review the entire
body of research concerning social learning in infancy, a representative sampling
of three indices of social responsiveness

will be attempted: (1) touching, (2) smiling, and (3) vocalizing. These appear to be three areas logically playing an important role in fostering adult-infant interactions as well as the development of social attachments. Also, these indices automatically incorporate proximity, paying attention, and affectionate behavior. In addition, it is upon this research focus that Bijou and Baer built their empirical theory of child development.

According to Wolff (1963), between the third and eighth week social smiling begins. Although Wolff's findings were photographically documented, he admits that observing the subject at home with the mother present and with her competing for evoking social smiles possibly increased social responsiveness. Wolff's research does indicate, however, that a combination of voice and face, particularly a moving face, is the most reliable elicitor of smiling early in the infant's life.

Brackbill (1958), using operant conditioning procedures, increased the frequency of smiling behavior in three-month-old infants. She also demonstrated that intermittently reinforced infants smiled at a higher rate during extinction than continuously reinforced infants.

Wahler (1967), in studying conditioned smiling--also in three-month-old infants--compared the reinforcing effectiveness of mothers and strangers as dispensers of visual, auditory, and tactual stimulation. Reliable increases in smiling occurred during conditioning when the infant's mother dispenses reinforcement but not when the female stranger served as the reinforcing agent.

Etzel and Gewirtz (1967), in a study

of conditioned smiling using social reinforcement but excluding physical contact,
indicated that a combination of visual and
auditory stimulation is sufficient to ob-
tain reliable reinforcement effects in infants as young as six weeks of age.

Weisberg (1963) convincingly demonstrated that (1) vocalizing could be op-
erantly conditioned in young infants and
(2) social stimulation is a more effective
reinforcer than nonsocial stimulation. His
subjects were thirty-three three-month-old
infants.

Rheingold et al. (1959), using a complex reinforcer--that is, smiling, talk-
ing, and contact--successfully increased
the frequency of vocalizations in three-
month-old infants. Rubenstein (1967) time-
sampled maternal attentiveness behavior,
using forty-four five-month-old infants.
Maternal attentiveness was defined as the
number of times the mother was observed to
look at, touch, hold, or talk to her baby.
At the end of one month, infants from the
high-attentiveness group significantly ex-
ceeded the low-attentiveness group in exploratory behavior.

Thus research clearly indicates that
the young infant's social behavior is
highly sensitive to social reinforcement
and that social reinforcement is effective
in strengthening and maintaining a number
of responses. As Hebb pointed out earlier,
the infant is not simply a passive recipient of stimulation. That the mother-infant
relationship is clearly reciprocal and
that the infant is capable of modifying
the behavior of others has been suffi-
ciently demonstrated by Moss and Robson
(1968). In their study, fifty-four mother-
infant pairs were observed in a six-hour

home visit of infants one month of age.
The frequency with which either mother or
infant initiated an interaction sequence
was recorded. In approximately four out of
five instances, it was the infant who initiated the interaction.

In view of the above, it can perhaps
now be logically accepted that not only
does preverbal behavior set the stage for
later social or interpersonal developmental characteristics, but in addition it can
be directly influenced and altered by maternal or caretaker interaction. In other
words, for some infants being touched,
cuddled, patted, and so on is practically
a way of life, and their reaction to these
stimuli is not only gratifying but sought
after as well. And, in addition, the speed
of development of social behavior such as
smiling and vocalizing as related to
cross-cultural variations is, no doubt,
contingent upon the caretaker interaction
common for a particular culture.

Reactions to another person's touch,
proximity, and so on stemming from early
neonatal interaction have obvious implications for parents and school teachers
who attempt to motivate and form positive
relationships with their charges. In fact,
it could very well be that during the
first few days and weeks of life social
learning forms the groundwork for all
later interpersonal relationships. Sidney
Jourard (1968), representing contemporary
humanistic psychologists, states that now-
adays touching the average person on the
arm or placing one's arm around another's
shoulder often results in that individual
stiffening, experiencing panic, jumping as
if stabbed, and perhaps even experiencing
a mixture of sexual arousal and guilt. Al-

though possibly exaggerated, Jourard's statements are well taken in light of the present Zeitgeist. In the face of our present-day technological society, techniques of promoting humanness must be sought after. Is there a more appropriate place to begin humanness than during the first days of life?

The question now arises as to the validity in assuming a generalization effect in terms of application of early social learning to disadvantaged school-age children, children usually thought of as victims of weak social reinforcement histories.

Baron (1970) has suggested a model of the effects of differences in social reinforcement history that has relevance to observations made by Dreger and Miller (1968). That is, poor children receive smaller amounts of positive social reinforcement because (1) "the mother spends more time coping with her child's behavior rather than shaping it and (2) the mother devotes all her time to subsistence activities, e.g., working at menial jobs" (1968, p. 19).

Baron's (1970) model assumes "the existence of an incongruity sensitive mechanism which is rooted in the individual's past reinforcement history and is an important determinant of his present receptivity to social reinforcing" (p. 61). Baron refers to a

preferred region around which the individual seeks to secure future social reinfocement as that individual's social reinforcement standard (SRS). In regard to the disadvantaged and especially Negro youth the SRS model has special relevance to the problems of how to improve the motivation and performance of the poor because it suggests that we must not assume that types and levels of reinforcement which are effective with more affluent subject populations will be effective with the poor. For example, it follows from the SRS model that Negroes would find a low rate of approval from a white authority figure more appropriate and preferred than a high rate of approval (pp. 65-66).

In discussing the general responsiveness in social situations, Schaffer and Emerson (1964) postulate a varying threshold of responsiveness which they refer to as a social sensitivity factor; this concept seems appropriately analogous to Baron's incongruity sensitive mechanism. Bijou and Baer (1965) refer to this phenomenon as "attending variability."

In reference to Baron's model, one might possibly question the validity of assuming a typical disadvantaged child. Beiser (1965) points out that "certain aspects of personality functioning among the disintegrated poor emerge with sufficient clarity and frequency that they demand attention" (p. 58). He classifies these aspects as (1) personal traits, such as lack of future orientation and inability to defer gratification, apathy, and suspiciousness; (2) level of skills (inadequate); and (3) the state of psychological well-being (poor).

According to Sears et al. (1957), lower-class mothers have been found to be emotionally colder to their children.

Hollingshead and Redlich (1958) report that a "loveless infancy" is more common in lower-class families than those in the middle class. Phillips (1968), in studying older children, states that a sense of right and wrong is not strongly internalized in lower-class and slum children and that behavioral trends are controlled mainly by the fear of being caught and punished rather than by feelings of guilt. The implication is an underlying disrespect for and suspicion of all authority, masked by superficial conformity. In relation specifically to Rubenstein's (1967) study cited above, Klaus and Gray (1968) report that mothers of disadvantaged children reward behaviors that leave them alone rather than encourage exploratory behavior. There is no extensive literature that relates earlier family experiences within the various social classes to later personality development. Research is needed to determine if there exists actual measurable differences in middle-class and disadvantaged mother-infant dyads, specifically in terms of stimulus-response-reinforcement contingencies. Studies such as those reported by Rubenstein, Brackbill (1958) and Wahler (1967) need to be replicated with special attention to social-class and racial differences. The major focus of future research, however, must be upon longitudinal studies and the question of stability or retention of early operant behaviors over time.

In terms of dealing with the child well beyond Erikson's trust stage, Beiser suggests, for example, the utilization of peer relationships in shaping social responsiveness and motivations, since this

type of relationship may be more support-
ive and less threatening. This, however,
is but one specific suggestion for increasing motivation. Needless to say, this
chapter does not propose that child victims of weak social reinforcement histories are not amenable to behavior change.

Common to Hebb, Erikson, and Bijou
and Baer, there appears to be an inner
population of remembered and anticipated
sensations that are firmly related to the
outer population of familiar and predictable things and people. Whether these are
termed cell assemblies, interpersonal relationships, or reinforcement histories
depends upon one's theoretical orientation. Not only does it seem logical that
environmental or caretaker variables, in
the neonatal period, significantly affect
later behavior, but that the manipulation
of these variables can be accomplished by
operant or social learning techniques resulting in totally unique human beings in
terms of social interaction and responsiveness later in life. (See the discussion in the introduction to this section
regarding Bindra's (1974) incentive-
motivational theory of learning and
Estes's (1972) informational feedback
theory.)

In an attempt to make more real the
components of trust described in the pre-
ceding section, the specific components or
ideas discussed will be structured into
overt demonstrable behaviors (see Madsen
and Madsen (1970). The politics of initiating a program of positive mother-
infant interactions in disadvantaged
groups will not be attempted. Blackham and
Silberman (1971), for example, stressed
the fact that the relevant question in re-

gard to initiating behavior change programs is how much parents, teachers, and
other significant persons are willing to
give of their time. Research designed to
answer this important question is certainly required prior to the formulation and
implementation of change strategies and
logically follows on the heels of empirical evidence--longitudinal--in regard to
cultural differences in mother-infant relationships as discussed earlier.

In specific mother-child (and/or
father-child) dyads, clearly stated defi-
nitions of behaviors are required. In addition, a systematic analysis of behaviors
is required. And a systematic analysis of
behaviors by careful observation and baseline data collection should be accomplished. Examples of specific behaviors
necessary to produce optimal positive social learning experiences and subsequently
strong reinforcement histories are listed
in table 1. It should be noted that these
ideas do not include all possible behaviors included in mother-infant interaction
patterns.

After recording behaviors, attempts
should then be made to initiate interactional changes if, according to a prede-
termined decision, baseline data is below
that previously judged adequate. For example, data could be collected from those
mother-infant dyads whose interactional
patterns have been empirically determined as adequately fostering positive social learning strategies.

A major assumption made by this
writer is that mothers are interested in
relating to their children in as positive
a manner as possible. For this reason, reinforcement contingencies aimed at chang-

ing the behavior of unwilling mothers have
not been discussed.

Table 1

Behaviors	Counted across
A. Idea: Proximity	
1. Mother-infant within two feet or less of each other (v)[1]	_____ hours
2. Actual physical contact (v)	_____ hours
B. Idea: Paying Attention	
1. Looking at (v)	_____ hours
2. Turning to (v)	_____ hours
3. Facial change (v)	_____ hours
C. Idea: Affection Toward	
1. Smiling (v)	_____ hours
2. Kissing (v)	_____ hours
3. Hugging (v)	_____ hours
4. Patting (v)	_____ hours
5. Making pleasant sounds (v) (a)[2]	_____ hours

1. Observed visually.
2. Observed aurally.

5. SOCIAL DEVELOPMENT

C. Etta Walters and Patricia Wilhoit

Once the road to contact with the human partner has opened for the infant it will pursue it regardless of disappointments and obstacles with the incredible tenacity which characterizes the urge to live.

Spitz (1946)

Anna Freud (1968) has written that the young child, when driven by his instinctual impulses, is uncivilized, primitive, selfish, aggressive, and immodest. She says he has no powers of self-control and no experience to guide him; his desire is to seek pleasure and to avoid pain. She says "The task of shaping out of this raw material the future members of a civilized society lies above all with the parents" (p. 470).

It is the purpose of this chapter to discuss the ways in which the child--this primitive, uncivilized, selfish being--is changed, in the first twelve to eighteen months of life, into what hopefully will

99

become a civilized, unselfish, modest, altruistic human being.

It is not the purpose of this discussion to make an issue between ethological (Bowlby 1958) or psychoanalytic theory concerning the social development of the infant. Anna Freud (1969), in her discussion of John Bowlby's work, writes that both agree that the infant becomes attached to his mother as a result of primary biological urges that ensure survival. Bowlby's concept of a biological tie that results in certain behavioral patterns is paralleled, she says, by the psychoanalytic concept of "an inborn readiness to cathect with libido a person who provides pleasurable experiences" (p. 176).

The terms object relations, dependency, and attachment have been used in various theoretical formulations of the origin and development of the infant's social relations. They are not synonymous, but there is a great deal of basic similarity among them. "Object relations" comes from psychoanalysis and is defined as the agent through which the instinctual aim is achieved. This object is generally thought of as being the infant's mother. Social learning theorists use the term" "dependency" to describe the origin and development of the infant's interpersonal relations. There are two prevailing views of dependency. One group sees dependency as a secondary drive occurring because the mother has gratified the infant's basic physiological needs--his primary drives. The other group views dependency as a learned behavior linked to a nurturant mother. Nurturance, in this instance, is broadened to include stimulation and help

in controlling the environment. "Attachment" is used by ethologists and is defined as an affectionate, discriminative,
interactive relationship with another person (Ainsworth 1964, 1969; Bowlby 1958).

What these disciplines have in common
is their shared interest in the origin and
development of the infant's first interpersonal relations. The psychoanalytic
point of view holds that cathexis with the
libidinal object occurs because the object
has gratified the infant's primary needs;
thus it centers around orality. The social
learning theorists who see dependency as
learned behavior reject the secondary
drive theory. They tend to think of environment as all-important and to disregard
inner structure. The infant's behavior is
conditioned by the mother providing positive reinforcement to the infant and with-
drawing negative reinforcement. The ethologists (Ainsworth, Bowlby, Schaffer, and
others) feel that the infant's behavior
comes about through the interaction of
those aspects of his environment that his
constitution is sensitive to receive. They
view attachment as an inner representation
(once formed, it can withstand separation)
that can be measured only by behaviors
they refer to as "attachment behavior."
Ethologists conceive of the organism
starting with a number of highly structured species-specific responses which, in
the course of development, become more
complex through learning, imitation, identification, and the use of symbols. To
them, attachment is an innate, social need
occurring as a result of the above-mentioned characteristics, which tend to bind
child to mother and vice versa (Ainsworth
1969, Bowlby 1958, Schaffer and Emerson

1964).

In the last decade, most of the research on the early interpersonal relations of the infant has been directed toward the study of the development of attachment. Animal studies such as the one by Harlow and Harlow (1966) have supported this theory. They found that rhesus monkeys provided with gratification of their physiological needs but deprived of maternal contact demonstrated deviant personality development. In later life, they in turn proved to be fairly inept at providing their young with good mothering. A psychoanalyst, John Bowlby, was the leader in formulating this new approach to interpersonal relations in the human infant. This chapter will confine its discussion of this aspect of the socialization of the infant to the psychoanalytic frame of reference and to the theory of attachment.

Socialization implies the interaction of one being with another/others. At birth and for several weeks thereafter, no ego, and therefore no superego, exists. The infant is viewed as existing in an undifferentiated state (Hartman 1939) or, as Spitz (1965) prefers, a nondifferentiated state. At this time the infant does not distinguish between mind and body, between outside and inside, between "I" and "non-I," or even between various parts of the body (Spitz 1965).

Mother and infant exist in a stage of symbiosis (see the social symbiosis section in chapter I). From this stage of oneness the infant gradually learns that things exist outside of himself. Through touch, proprioception, kinesthesis, vission, and other modalities, he comes to

feel that he is not one amorphous mass,
identical with and indistinguishable from
all others in the universe. All of the
above-mentioned ways of distinguishing
self from nonself are aided by the association with his mother. Spitz (1965) won-
ders why sociologists have ignored the opportunity to observe the mother-infant relationship and see the beginning and evolution of social relations *in statu
nascendi*.

Thus object relations originate in
the early mother-infant relationship, and
in the beginning no object or object relations, hence no attachments, exist for the
newborn infant.

In the process of gradually learning
that objects, both animate and inanimate,
exist outside of himself, the infant also
learns to become attached to someone.

Cairns (1972) has summarized for us
the focus of what we believe should be emphasized regarding attachment. He has
written that the issue is not whether
"biophysical events influence behavior"
nor "whether evolutionary factors or survival properties" are implicated in the
predilection of a human being to form relationships. The issue is, he believes--as
do we--that we have to answer some questions concerning the stability of social
interaction patterns and deal with some of
the exact mechanisms that influence it.

While digressing some from the questions he says need to be answered regarding attachment, we find Cairns's views a
convenient springboard from which to discuss the various facets of socialization
in infancy.

SOCIALIZING AGENTS

First, we take the position Rheingold (1971) does, that is, the infant is a social being from birth; and second, that mother-infant interaction is essential in this process.

The sight of social objects evokes responses from the infant almost from birth (Rheingold 1966). Bowlby (see Ainsworth 1969) feels that infants have an in-built bias toward looking at certain patterns and at things that move, which predisposes them to pay special attention to the human face. Wolff (1963) sees eye-to-eye contact as relevant for the development of smiling, because in his study, by the fourth week, next to vocalization, eye-to-eye contact was the most efficient stimulus in eliciting a smile from the infant. Wolff also found evidence that eye-to-eye contact elicits maternal social behavior; a couple of the mothers in his study began spending more time playing with their infants a few days after their babies established eye-to-eye contact with them. Schaffer and Emerson (1964) found that about the middle of the first year situations in which visually maintained contact was interrupted elicited the most protest from the infant. Robson (1967) feels that contact is basic to human socialization and if not established, or if of an insufficient quality, the infant will experience varying degrees of difficulty in forming specific attachments.

ROLE OF STIMULI

What are the stimuli that initiate social interaction? Basic to this question is the assumption that all organisms need and seek stimulation (Hebb 1955). The literature abounds with studies of the results of perceptual deprivation. Schneirla (1965) has published an illuminating article in which he proposes approach (A) and withdrawal (W)--the A-W process--are two basic biological responses which through evolution gradually have become "seeking" and "avoidance," thus making them more biopsychological than biophysiological. This process, present in animals, is repeated in the early stages of human infancy.

In the neonate, rooting, sucking, and grasping responses are of low intensity and bring gratification; they are clasical approach processes that involve the parasympathetic system. They are responses to stimuli of low intensity. Loud noises and other stimuli of high intensity produce withdrawal responses, such as the Moro or startle response, and are effected through the sympathetic nervous system.

The infant's equipment for W responses is limited and inadequate compared to those for A responses (Schur, 1960). He does not have the means to eliminate the effects of intensive stimulation.

It would therefore seem that these early responses (rooting, sucking, and grasping), initiated by the infant, evoke

pleasurable tactual responses in the mother, and and are the beginnings of socialization. Other stimuli, such as crying,
smiling, are all initiated by the infant
and produce responses by the mother, and
so a circular reaction by which mother
and infant interact in a gratifying experience results (see the introduction to
this section).

The social smile which Wolff (1963)
has observed as early as the third week is
responsive to the high-pitched voice of a
human being. However, the average age for
the appearance of the social smile is
about eight weeks. While auditory stimuli
are the first to elicit the social smile
(Wolff), the human face follows soon after
as an important evoker of the smile.

Discrimination to various stimuli
occurs through many receptors (see chapters 7 and 8) and probably through some-
esthetic modalities before others (see the
discussion of Spitz's coenesthetic organization in the introduction to section 1).
By seven months, plus or minus, the infant
becomes more discriminating in his responses to humans, and he more clearly
differentiates one object (human) from
another. In this manner he becomes attached to a person, which in most cases is
his mother. However, the infant may be attached to others as well in his environment (Ainsworth 1972, Bowlby 1958, Spitz
1965).

Cohen and Campos (1974), in testing
infants ten, thirteen, and sixteen months
of age, found fathers were preferred to
strangers in proximity-seeking behaviors
and were preferred second to mothers when
both parents were present. Eye-to-eye contact with the mother was greater than be-

tween father and infant. Ban and Lewis
(1974) found one-year-old infants responded to mothers with proximal-
attachment (touching) behaviors and to
fathers with distancing attachment (looking) behaviors.

Contact stimulation has long been
recognized as providing the infant with
warmth and security and helping him to
differentiate between I and non-I
(Winnicott 1960, Escalona 1963). Schaffer
and Emerson (1964) described babies who
actively sought and enjoyed close, physical contact as "cuddlers" and those who
resist close, physical contact which re-
stricted their movement as "non-cuddlers."
They saw this preference or dislike of
close, physical contact to be a function
of basic personality rather than an accommodation, on the infant's part, to maternal handling. the "non-cuddlers" preferred to receive, and did receive, most
of their stimulation through the distance
receptors. Thus, we can see that the infant's unique constitution predisposes him
to seek stimulation from his environment
in a certain manner.

After studying cuddlers and non-
cuddlers, Schaffer and Emerson came to
the conclusion that what appears to matter
in the establishment of primary social
bonds is the total amount of stimulation
rather than any particular mode of stimulation. Schaffer and Emerson, Moss (1967),
and Ferguson (1971) have postulated that
the infant has a basic need for stimulation and that he learns that this need can
be gratified through social interaction.
Thus stimulation comes to serve as a basis
for relating to others. Schaffer and
Emerson found support for this position in

that some of the infants in their study were attached to individuals who provided no caretaking activities but a great deal of stimulation. This other person was most often the father who spent a limited but very stimulating period of time with the infant.

The "critical period" can be defined as a certain time period in development during which a particular class of stimuli will have a profound effect (Denenberg 1964; Frank 1966). Due to the more highly developed brain and thus greater flexibility of the human organism, it is more difficult to research critical periods in infants than it is in animals. This is not to say that certain periods do not exist. Caldwell (1962) and Ambrose (1963) believe there are critical periods in human filiative behavior. They see visual pursuit as comparable to the following-response seen in certain animals; both serve to bring the infant close to his mother.

The role of maternal care seems to follow logically a discussion of critical periods in the infant's psychological development. It is through his mother that the infant comes to recognize and to learn about his world and about himself. Object relations that gratify both infant and mother mediate ego development, the quality of later object relations, and basic early orientations such as trust. The mother must, in the beginning, serve as the infant's auxiliary ego, but as he matures she must allow him the independence he is capable of handling while remaining nearby to provide emotional support. For the infant to navigate successfully the critical periods of development, he must have a loving, trustworthy, need-satisfying libidinal object (Erikson 1950, Escalona 1968, Mahler 1968, Spitz 1965, Winnicott 1960).

How the mother will interact with her infant depends on her personality, her maternal feelings, and on her infant's unique temperament. This interaction between temperament and environment shapes the infant's personality (Thomas et al. 1970, Caldwell 1964) and influences his social development.

Moss (1967) found that mothers responded in a differential manner to their infants on the basis of age, sex, and state (activity level). Male infants cried more and, as a result, were held more; however, the social behavior of females was reinforced more because they responded more favorably to maternal social overtures. Robson and Moss (1970) studied maternal attitudes before and after delivery and found a positive correlation between maternal feelings of love, devotion, and concern for the infant and the degree of maternal attachment to the infant.

Osotsky and Danzer (1974) investigated fifty-one mother-infant pairs and found newborns who were most alert and responsive to auditory cues (as assessed by the Brazelton Neonatal Behavioral Assessment Scale) looked at the mother a great deal more during feeding observations. They also found that the attentive, sensitive mother responded to her responsive baby, and vice versa, demonstrating again the interaction process of mother-infant in socialization.

Beckwith (1972) found that mothers who were critical and suppressive in their behavior had less responsive babies who did not play with them.

FAILURES OF SOCIALIZATION

Aichhorn (1925), in his classic book *Wayward Youth*, saw disturbances and separations of the early parent-child relationship as responsible factors in creating delinquency states. He said:

> The formation of a socially directed ego-ideal cannot take place if the nucleus of the ego-ideal, which, as you know, is based on the first great love objects, is weak or nonexistent. Furthermore, object cathexis and identification require time to establish themselves (p. 226).

Bowlby (1944) studied forty-four juvenile delinquents and found that out of fourteen diagnosed as of "affectionateless character," twelve had been separated from their mothers in infancy.

The literature is replete with case histories of disturbances in the early mother-infant relationship. Whether it is from maternal rejection, separation, neglect, or abuse, the adverse effects of these disturbances often do not make their appearance until preadolescence or adolescence or at times of unusual stress.

Spitz (1965) has beautifully expressed the results of disturbed object relations:

> From the societal aspect, disturbed object relations in the first year of life, be they deviant, improper, or insufficient, have consequences which imperil the very foundation of society. Without a template, the vic-

tims of disturbed object relations
subsequently will themselves lack the
capacity to relate. . . . Infants
without love, they will end as adults
full of hate (p. 300).

6. INFANT DAY CARE

Clayton E. Stumpff

Quis custodiet ipsos custodes?

In 1964 approximately 10 percent of all the world's infants were in day-care or week-care centers or in full-time institutions (World Health Organization 1964). In 1972 Caldwell reported that in the United States the increasing number of infants and toddlers under three years of age in group day care was due in part to the increasing number of women in the labor force. She stated that in June 1958, 883,000 mothers with children under three were in the labor force. By March 1967, this number had increased to 1,024,000. This put the number of infants and toddlers in group care at 49,000. With an increase in momentum of the women's liberation movement, the work force continues to grow daily. Also, the encouragement of teen-age mothers to keep their babies, married or not, and to finish high school is adding to the need for infant day care. Can adequate care be provided for infants in a day-care setting?

Provence (1967) has stated that most
infants--at least 90 percent--are born
with the capacity to develop normally, but
they must be cared for in a way so that
development is supported and not inter-
fered with. She says that each infant
needs personalized care. This refers to
being cared for by a person who can love
and be interested in the baby as well as
answer his specific needs. Ribble (1943)
calls this "mother love." She says that
every infant has a right to mother love;
without it, or if care is impersonal, the
baby's mental development will be impaired.

Ribble has also pointed out that
mothering involves many thing; giving attention to the infant's biological needs,
providing physical care, attending to psychological needs, as well as providing
adequate sensory stimulation. Can day care
provide all of this?

The purpose of this chapter will be
to try to answer this question by discussing some of the various aspects of the
infant day-care setting including the
separation of the child from his mother
and the environment that must be provided
for infant day care--physical and, most
important, social-emotional.

THE SEPARATION

Caldwell (1972) recently stated that
day care, by definition, has meant the
separation of the child and his mother.
And for the past twenty years, maternal
separation has equaled maternal deprivation, with its greatest effects on the

child under three. This separation-
deprivation equality has been documented
by studies of institutionalized infants
(Goldfarb 1943 and Spitz 1945).

It has also been pointed out that
deprivation and separation are not necessarily the same thing (Yarrow 1961, 1964).
This seems rather obvious by the defini-
tions given by Ainsworth (1962) of maternal deprivation and separation. Dr.
Ainsworth defines "maternal deprivation"
as a situation in which an infant or
young child is reared for a more or less
prolonged period of time under conditions
that provide him with inadequate maternal
care and insufficient interaction with a
mother figure. "Separation," she says, refers to the physical separation of the infant or young child from his mother regardless of the length of the period of
time. She adds that maternal deprivation
can occur in the absence of separation,
and separation can occur in the absence of
deprivation of maternal care.

Even though separation and maternal
deprivation may not necessarily be the
same thing, the importance of the early
attachment of the infant to mother or a
substitute mother (Spitz 1946, Bowlby 1952,
Schaffer and Emerson 1964) still remains.
A review of the research by Yarrow (1964)
summarizes a number of critical factors
concerning temporary separation and the
mother-child relationship. One of these
factors is the age at the time of separation. It is stated that the attachment of
the child to his mother usually takes
place in the second half of the first
year. A separation before the attachment
is formed is less severe than separation
after the relationship is established. If

the separation is followed by the provis-
sion of an adequate mother-figure, there
may be no serious effect.

Yarrow also points out that the
quality of the mother-child relationship
prior to the separation is an important
factor. He says that although it has been
found that the most severe reactions to
separation are from those with the closest
relationships, the child with the strong
relationship may be able to tolerate the
separation better because he knows and
trusts that the mother will return. The
child with the strong relationship may also be able to establish a more meaningful
relationship with a substitute figure than
a child who has not experienced an inti-
mate relationship.

Maccoby (1958) has stated that the
child of a working mother may not suffer
any great degree of maternal deprivation,
because he has the love of the mother during a predictable portion of his waking
hours and has the love of the substitute
in her absence. She suggests that the real
problem for children of working mothers
lies in separation anxiety; that is, the
child is anxious each day because he feels
rejected and abandoned. Maccoby proposes
that to reduce this anxiety (1) the division of the caretaking responsibility
should become common practice, (2) the
daily departure should start in infancy
before the child is accustomed to one
caretaker, and (3) the substitute should
use the same techniques as the mother.

The mention of a substitute mother so
far has seemed to indicate a single individual who assumes the caretaking responsibilities while the mother is away.
Can this be accomplished in a group-care

situation? Can group care provide this one-to-one relationship needed by the child?

The goal of group care is to provide the infant with a person with whom he can form a close relationship (Provence 1967). This person or main caretaker is a supplement to the mother's own relationship with the child, or if there is a lack of a close mother-child relationship the child is provided with a caretaker with a personalized interest in him during the time he is in the center (Provence 1968).

Provence (1967) has said that since the child may mistrust the substitute at first, it may be helpful if the substitute is introduced by the mother. She also suggests that the child's fear of loss of the mother may be lessened by leaving a familial object, such as a stuffed animal or bottle, with the child. This is one way of coping with the stress.

The placing of an infant in group care has not been proven to have any harmful effects on the child (Swift 1964). Recent research by Caldwell et al. (1970 at the Children's Center in Syracuse, New York, has also shown no adverse effects from day care on the mother-child attachment. In this study, a group of children that had been in the center from early infancy and a group cared for at home by their mothers were compared on their thirtieth-month birthday. No significant differences were found between the groups as to the mother-child attachment or child-other relationships. In an investigation of the home characteristics of the children cared for by their mothers, an association was found between the amount of stimulation in the home and the intensity of the child's attachment to the mother.

This study gives support to the theory that damage does not always occur as a consequence of the separation experience; but it may result because an inappropriate human environment was provided for the child (Trosler 1968). This would indicate, then, that day care should direct its efforts toward providing the proper environment for the infant.

THE ENVIRONMENT

The environment, as described by Murphy (1968), contains many things that can influence the child's sensory, cognitive, and motor development. Provence (1968) discusses a threefold concept of the determinants of a child's development that entails an interaction between the child's innate characteristics, his environment, and his stage of development. She says that in early infancy environment usually refers to the quantity and quality of maternal care. But as the child grows older, his world and his variety of experiences increase, and this also is his environment. This environment or experience, she says, must occur in the proper phase of the child's development. In interacting with his innate characteristics, it determines the child's development.

Provence point out that experiences which may be appropriate for one child because of his phase of development and his innate characteristics may be traumatic for another. But, she says, there are enough similarities in the needs and ca-

pacities of children of comparable ages,
living under comparable conditions, for
recommendations to be made as to how their
needs can be met. Thus environments can be
developed that will provide adequate care
of infants in groups.

It has been suggested (Gewirtz 1968)
that parents who put infants in group care
should train their children to control
their environment. This can be done by reinforcing the child's smiling and interesting vocal responses. These responses
will in turn elicit a response from the
caretaker, and thus the child can control
the caretaker, thereby controlling his environment. (See the introduction to part
II of this book for a critique of reinforcement techniques.)

The specifics of the day-care environment might be more easily discussed in
sections. Therefore the remainder of the
discussion of the environment will be focused on the physical environment, the
social-emotional environment, and the
staff.

The Physical Environment

It is necessary for the day-care environment to provide adequate nourishment
for the child's growth and health. It
should also provide for the prevention of
physical illness through protective measures (Provence 1967, 1968).

Caldwell (1972) has written that in-
oculations have ended the terror of polio
and smallpox epidemics, but she predicts
that infants kept daily in group care will
have runny noses and respiratory infec-

tions. She describes the Frank Porter
Graham Center in Chapel Hill, North
Carolina. This is a federally funded center recently established for a thirteen-
year longitudinal study of the effects of
infant day care. Reports from this center
have shown that the average incidence of
respiratory illness was 8.9 per year for
children one year of age and 10 per year
for children under one year of age. Compared to a study of children in a metro-
politan area, the figure was 8.3 for illness in children under one year of age and
7.4 for children from two to five.

Caldwell felt that this indicated
that the health of the infants was not
significantly impaired by constant exposure to large groups of children. She
added that the children at the Frank
Porter Graham Center attended whether they
were well or sick. They were not isolated
unless it was best for the child. There is
excellent medical care at the center, and
very high standards of cleanliness are
maintained.

The World Health Organization (1964)
has suggested a number of health standards
that should be observed by day care centers:

1. Only healthy children should be
admitted to centers.

2. There should be a preadmission examination to exclude children who have
acute infectious diseases.

3. All staff members should have a
health examination to keep them from in-
fecting the children as well as for their
own well-being. The minimum requirement

should be a health certificate including a chest X-ray before beginning work.

4. Special attention should be given to the diets of infants. Preferably this should be prescribed by a pediatrician.

5. There should be an ample number of isolation rooms available for children who become ill during the day. It is recommended that there be one room for every fifteen to twenty children, and that these rooms be near the entrance and away from where the group spends the day.

6. Accident training should be included in any staff training program.

7. The health aspects of the center should be one of the major responsibilities of the director. The responsibility for the children's physical and mental health should rest on the entire staff.

The Child Welfare League of America (1969) has suggested similar health standards but adds that care should be taken to ensure that the building in which the center is located is structurally sound, free from fire hazards, and maintained in a sanitary condition.

One of the main concerns in the physical environment should be for space, says Murphy (1968). She writes that this should be considered in relation to the number of children involved and their needs for motor activity. Too often infants are kept in cribs that are crowded into a small area, and the crying of one or two infants sets off the crying of the others. No opportunity is available for

the exercise on the floor that a young infant enjoys. And if the room is monotonous
and bare, the infant is not offered enough
stimuli for the basic processes of differentiation or sensory gratification.

Toys and other playthings should also
be made available for infants, because
these offer stimulation and an outlet for
the release of feelings and aid in developing a sense of independence (Provence
1967, 1968). The World Health Organization
(1964) lists a number of toys appropriate
to the age of the child. These can be summarized as:

2-3 months: A rattle that is light,
not too big, washable, and unbreakable;
the color should preferably be red, since
red is discriminated early.

3-4 months: A row of celluloid or
plastic beads or a bright colored mobile
should be placed above the crib; and a
wooden holder for small objects that make
noise.

8 months: Unbreakable toys that the
child can hold, throw, and strike togeth-
er.

9-10 months: Affectionate toys like a
teddy bear and a rag doll.

10-15 months: Bright colored scraps
of cloth, paper for crumbling, containers
to fill and empty, spools to roll, and
plastic bottles to uncork for comparing
and exploring qualities of objects.

The Child Welfare League (1969)

stresses that floor space allotted to
floor play for infants should be covered
with a smooth and splinter proof material
that is easily cleaned, such as linoleum
or asphalt tile.

The Social-Emotional Environment

Provence (1967, 1968) has outlined
some specific experiences and forms of
stimulation that are appropriate to the
infant's development in a group-care setting. The most important of these is a
main or primary caretaker with a personalized interest in the child and with whom
the child can form a primary attachment.
This person also serves as a social speak-
ing partner. This is important for the
development of speech and the child's inner world of thought and general awareness.

Provence stresses that the atmosphere
should include a reasonable amount of consistency and repetition. It should be free
of major discomfort and tension so that
the child is able to give attention to
the people and things in his environment.
Too often, day care has excessive routini-
zation and rigidity in schedules. The
child should be given opportunities to
move about, to play, and to use his emerging skills and dispositions in a support-
ive and safe atmosphere. This aids the development of independence and self-
determination.

But within this atmosphere created by
consistency and repetition Provence suggests that there should be variety and
contrast in order to produce a mild tension

state that calls for an adaptive response.
There should be limits and prohibitions
appropriate to the age of the child; he
needs to experience tension, inner conflict, and frustration, since he will always have these in the process of education and socialization.

The research by Caldwell et al.
(1970) cited earlier indicates that a
proper social-emotional environment can be
created in a day-care setting. It was concluded from this research that the Children's Center in Syracuse, New York, had
provided an environment that would prevent any developmental detriment associated with maternal separation, and that
the environment was enriched to provide a
good growing and learning center for all
children. It must be remembered, though,
that the adult-child ratio was carefully
controlled, as was the entire range of experiences supplied for the children. More
research is planned in this longitudinal
study to determine if there are any long-
term effects of group care on the child.

In addition to the physical environment and the general atmosphere for
proper development, people also are an
important stimulus in the environment.
They can enhance or inhibit the development of the child (Murphy 1968). (See the
introductions to parts II and III of this
book for further critiques of separation,
deprivation, and multiple mothering.)

The Staff

The proper adult-child ratio for infant day care is one adult for every two

infants (Child Welfare League of America 1969). This may vary with the particular situation and should be considered within the needs of the particular center and children involved (Tronick 1972).

Mr. Tronich is the educational advisor to the Bromky-Heath Infant Day Care Center in Boston, Massachusetts. He says that in their center they have children ranging from three months to three years of age; each adult is assigned to one young infant, one toddler, and a three-year-old, giving them a one to three adult-child ratio. This, he says, is easier on the caretaker than trying to care for two to three young infants at one time. Tronich also states that their program is somewhat structured to increase the time a child spends with an adult on a one-to-one basis.

Not all day care has such a small adult-child ratio, and the concept of multiple mothering has been a major criticism of group care. Provence (1967) says that too many substitutes can be bad; this may disrupt development in feeding, sleeping, or physical health. It may also create apathy in social and emotional development, and it may delay speech development as well as the capacity to play. Most of all, though, it may disrupt the child's primary attachment.

Much of the research on multiple mothering has been done with kibbutz children in Israel (Rabin 1958, Bettelheim 1969, and Kohen-Raz 1968).

Rabin's study of kibbutz infants and ten-year-olds produced results that pointed consistently to a lower level of ego development of the kibbutz infants as compared to their nonkibbutz peers. Most

of the differences were due to retardation
as expressed on the personal-social scale,
which involves the social and interpersonal responsiveness of the infant. The kibbutz ten-year-olds were superior to their
nonkibbutz peers in ego and intellectual
functions.

On the positive side, it has been
stated (Messinger 1965) that more kibbutz-
raised children are chosen for positions
of leadership during their compulsory two-
year military service than are nonkibbutz
children. Kohen-Raz also points to positive gains in mental and motor development
of kibbutz children.

Wolins (1970) reported on a study of
group care settings in Austria, Israel,
Poland, and Yugoslavia. The children in
these settings were tested on intellectual, personality, and value development.
In general, the group-reared children
showed no intellectual or psychological
deficiencies when compared with children
reared at home.

The controversy of multiple-mothering
still goes on, but so must the care of infants. As Provence (1967) notes, this can
be drudgery at times. In a personal note
to caretakers, she states that hopefully
caretakers can enjoy interaction between
the child and themselves. She hopes that
the outlining of environments and appropriate stimulation will not inhibit caretakers from being spontaneous and letting
themselves express their feelings. She
says that the giving of yourself to the
infant can increase your own self-esteem
and allow you to enjoy work that may con-
tain a number of unpleasant aspects.

THE EFFECTS OF THE DAY-CARE ENVIRONMENT ON DEVELOPMENT

In a recent article, Klein (1972) stated that infants cannot be left in their cribs to learn for themselves because attitudes are formed in cribs as well as on playgrounds. This seems to imply that the child can learn in any environment whether it be positive learning or negative learning.

Results of research at the Frank Porter Graham Child Development Center in Chapel Hill, North Carolina (Robinson and Robinson, 1971) point to significant gains in mental development for infants in day care. The study was conducted to assess the development of the eleven children who entered the center in 1966 and the twenty children who entered in 1967 and 1968. The children entered as early as one month and as late as twenty-eight months. A control group was used that was observed from infancy, as were some children who matched the ages of the older children. The controls were matched for sex, race, number of siblings, education and occupation of parents, and the number of rooms per house. For the subjects admitted as infants, a significant trend was found only on the mental scale. Both groups recorded an initial rise and then, at eighteen months, the control group began to drop. In the older children, the only significant findings were for the culturally deprived children. This led the authors to suggest that intervention needs to begin before eighteen months, and if carefully planned, it may enhance cognitive development.

Fowler (1972) reported on a three-year study undertaken to examine the significance of early experience as a critical period for developmental learning through a group day-care program of educational value for infants. The program was for working mothers and families in poverty whose children would benefit from the educational program. The project was a joint effort of the Ontario Institute for Studies in Education research group and the teaching staff and students of the Canadian Mother-Craft Society.

The children in the study ranged in age from two to thirty months at admission. There were thirty advantaged children and nine disadvantaged children. They were matched with a control group of home-reared infants.

The environment of the day-care program was based on developmental principles believed to be applicable to all children regardless of developmental level or background. The total program included student education, parent education, and the infant program.

The findings of this study on mental development showed a significant gain for the advantaged children but not for the disadvantaged children. While the gains were large and favorable for the advantaged day-care infants versus the home-reared controls, gains were not statistically significant. A correlation was found between early entry and longevity in the program and cognitive gain.

In social-emotional development, the scores on the Bayley Infant Behavior Record were consistently higher for the day-care group than for the home-reared infants. The disadvantaged infants showed

significant improvements in both inquisi-
tiveness and monotonous behavior during
play. The disadvantaged children had the
only negative evaluations in the ratings
in belligerence and irritability.

Evaluation of motor development
showed small gains for advantaged children and moderate gains for disadvantaged
children. The gain of the disadvantaged
was close to significant.

The findings of the two studies discussed in this section, plus the study of
the Children's Center in Syracuse, New
York (Caldwell et al. 1970) seem to indicate that group day cay can have a positive effect on infants. At least there
have been no significant negative findings
so far.

It should be pointed out, though,
that these are all highly controlled,
well-staffed centers designed for research
in infant day care. As Caldwell (1972) reported, programs that have a research component also have a cost of $2,400 to
$8,000 per year per child. An earlier re-
port of the center in Syracuse (Caldwell
and Richmond 1968) stated that without the
research component, the cost is still
high. Their original annual budget (without research) was $210,000, of which 90
percent went for salaries. This worked out
to a per child, per day cost of $11.54.
This means that good infant day care costs
more than commercial centers are willing
to spend and more than most parents are
willing to pay. Therefore, government-
funded centers appear to be the only way
to provide good infant day care.

SUMMARY AND CONCLUSION

This chapter has reviewed some of the various aspects of infant day care. It has pointed to the fact that the separation of the mother and child for day care may not result in maternal deprivation such as has often been found in the institutional care of infants. The development of a proper environment for the infant was outlined with a number of practical suggestions given. Research was also cited that indicates that no harmful effects have resulted from infant day care. In fact, the recent research has pointed only to positive effects on the development of the infant.

More research, however, is certainly necessary in the area of infant day care. Hopefully the funded centers mentioned that are designed for longitudinal studies will be able to bring out any long-term harmful effects. This is especially important in light of the cost figures presented, since it will require a considerable investment on the part of the government to provide good infant day care where necessary.

PART III

PERCEPTUAL-COGNITIVE DEVELOPMENT

This section is concerned with the mother-infant interaction that influences perceptual-cognitive development in infancy. Dr. Baker discusses the importance of stimulation in infancy and describes the types of stimuli and the influence of maternal, passive, and active stimulus barriers on the infant. Dr. Abu Nasr discusses various methods of studying perception of various modalities in infancy and reviews research studies dealing with the time of their occurrence in the infant. Dr. Ro focuses on the role of the mother in effecting the perceptual-cognitive development of her infant.

INTRODUCTION TO PART III

C. Etta Walters

> The more a child has seen and heard,
> The more he wants to see and hear.
>
> *Piaget (1952)*

Perception is intimately tied to cognition. It is more than the mere pouring of sensory impulses into an inactive brain; it involves the brain's "active and specific adjustment" (Sperry 1952). Sperry says that if there is anything demonstrable about perception that tells us something about the neural process involved, it is the followig: "In so far as an organism perceives an object, it is prepared to respond with reference to it. This preparation-to-respond is absent in an organism that has failed to perceive" (p. 415). We also have a tendency to see what we are looking for.

Sperry (1955) believes physiological theories have been prone to neglect this important element in conditioning, that is, the so-called anticipatory set or "ex-

pectancy." The neural counterparts of expectancy, he says, are high levels of central facilitation. Regarding this, he comments:

> It is by means of differential fa-
> cilitory sets that the brain is able
> to function as many machines in one,
> setting and resetting itself dozens
> of times in the course of a day, now
> for one type of operation, now for
> another. In short, a great deal of
> the plasticity in vertebrate behav-
> iour, including that of conditioning,
> is made possible, not through struc-
> tural remodeling of the fibre path-
> ways, but through dynamic readjust-
> ments in the background of central
> facilitation (pp. 42-43).

Walter (1965) has demonstrated by
electroencephalography the neural process
involved when the organism is prepared to
respond by associated stimuli. This is
shown in the brain as a slow negative
"wave of expectancy" called an E-wave. In
children E-waves are not so easily evoked;
and in children under eight years of age,
they do not appear readily unless the
associated stimulus is supported by an appropriate suggestion and encouragement
(Walter 1964).

Regarding perception, Lashley (1954)
has pointed out the fact that we are never
aware of the integrative activity of the
brain while it progresses, and that things
perceived are always a consequence of pre-
ceding and complex integrative processes.

When one attends to a stimulus, the
orienting reflex (OR), which was first described in 1910 by Pavlov (Pavlov 1927)

and termed the "what is it" or investigatory reflex, is evoked. The OR brings
about changes not only in the CNS--among
which is a desynchronization of the rest-
ing alpha waves--but in visceral, somatic,
and neural reactions as well. All of these
increase the discriminatory ability of the
analyzers and provide more information
concerning the stimulus.

The orientation reflex awakens and
alerts the brain to the specific stimulus
so that it can be identified by the brain
upon its arrival there. The anatomical
structure responsible for this arousal is
the brain stem reticular formation, first
described as such by Morruzi and Magoun
(1949). They demonstrated that stimulation
of the reticular formation caused the
above-mentioned changes to occur in the
cortex. They called it the reticular
arousing system (ARS). Magoun (1963) says
this arousal pattern "is identical with,
or forms part of the Pavlovian orienting
of investigatory reflex" (p. 109).

It is not the purpose here to describe other structures of the reticular
formation (midbrain formation) that par-
ticipate in the arousal pattern,[1] except
to point out that the brain itself can
control the arousal system, thereby influencing its own level of activation. This
is made possible by descending cortical
projections to the brain stem reticular
structure and the thalamic nuclei.

Sokolov (1960) has proposed a cortical neuronal model to explain the OR produced by novel stimuli. The neuronal model

---

1. An excellent review of the reticular
formation and behavior is given by Samuels
(1959).

is construed as a cortical cell assembly that retains information concerning earlier stimuli. Sokolov posits that whenever the aspects of the novel stimulus do not coincide with those of the model, the orienting reflex is evoked. However, when model and stimulus complex are in accord the OR is not induced. As the model becomes familiar, the OR habituates or shifts to other aspects of the stimuli.

Hebb (1955) points out that there are two different results of a sensory "event." One is the cue function that guides behavior and the other the arousal function without which cue function cannot exist. Hebb describes an inverted U-shaped curve to demonstrate the effect of too little or too much arousal. When the RAS is at a low level, a cue response that increases stimulation and greater arousal has a tendency to be repeated; however, when arousal is high, further stimulation may interfere with cue function by possibly facilitating irrelevant cues that can distract.

Leuba (1955) says evidence points to the fact that the concept of optimal stimulation enjoys wide application in human development. He comments:

> The organism tends to acquire those reactions which, when over-all stimulation is low, are accompanied by increasing stimulation, and when overall stimulation is high, those which are accompanied by decreasing stimulation (p. 29).

Jeffrey (1969), relying on a serial habituation hypothesis, analyzed the part habituation plays in attending responses.

He says as the OR habituates to a salient-
cue, new cues are attended to; or when the
OR has recovered from habituation, the old
cue is attended to. Finally, with repeated
exposure and more rapid habituation, attending responses become integrated into a
continuous response sequence. It is this
integration of a pattern of attending response and the habituation of that pattern
with other attending responses that defines an object percept or a schema.
Jeffrey says, "This analysis predicts that
an object schema can develop only in relatively variable context" (p 326). In an
environment composed of too many high-
salient cues, attention to the lesser features of the object would probably not occur, and thus object schema would no doubt
be delayed because of attending to the
high-priority cues. An object consisting
of too few salient-cues would not include
the variety needed for due stimulus response. Jeffrey sums up the above situation in the following way:

> In other words, when there are very
> few cues in a stimulus complex, ha-
> bituation to the complex will occur
> quickly, but with greater numbers of
> cues, successive habituation of the
> OR to each cue in the complex will
> take sufficient time to permit the OR
> to the most salient cue in the com-
> plex to recover, thus causing the at-
> tending sequence to be repeated (p.
> 328).

Yarrow et al. (1972), in a study of
dimensions of early stimulation and their
differential effects on infant development, found variety to be correlated with

infant measures dealing with inanimate objects and more highly correlated than was
complexity or responsiveness. Variety was
also the only variable of the three to
correlate significantly with cognitive
functions, for example, problem solving
(r = .50, p < .01) and object permanence
(r = .30, p < .05). As was expected, variety of inanimate objects showed a significant correlation (r = .48, p < .01) with
exploratory behavior.

Kagan (1972), in an interesting article entitled "Do Infants Think?" described experiments with babies using
change in heart rate as an orienting or
attending measure (decrease in heart rate
as infant attends) and as a thinking measure (increase in heart rate as the infant
thinks). He came to the conclusion that
infants' "cognitive hypothesis-forming development begins at the age of nine
months" (p. 72).

Lewis (1967), using habituation as an
index of cognitive growth, tested the hypothesis that cognitive development is facilitated by mother-infant interaction.
He found, in general, that rate of habituation was related to maternal responses
and was independent of the activity level
of the infant, thereby confirming his hypothesis.

Clarke-Stewart (1973), studying the
interaction of mothers and their firstborn
children (ages nine to eighteen months),
found the child's overall competency to be
significantly related to maternal care.
She felt that the investigation demonstrated "the importance of the mother as a
mediator of the physical environment" (p.
93).

Rosenzweig (1966) reported research

in which he and his colleagues, in well-
controlled experiments, subjected a group
of rats to an enriched environment and
their littermates to an impoverished environment. On the eightieth day, the rats
were taken from their cages and killed
and their brains removed and analyzed. The
findings of importance were that the
brains of the enriched rats were heavier
and had an increased depth when compared
to their controls. While the total body
weight of the enriched rats was less than
that of the impoverished, the weight increase in the brain was in the cortical
area, the level of highest functioning,
and not in the brain as a whole; there was
also an increase in those areas of the
brain which were related to the experiences the rats received. In addition to
the weight increase in the cortical area,
there were chemical changes. This was reflected in an increase in acetycholines-
terase (AChE) and cholinesterase (ChE) in
the cortex of the enriched rats. There was
also an increase in glial cells, which are
thought to nourish nerve cells, of the enriched cortex and an increase in the diam-
eter of the capillaries in the cortex of
the enriched rat.

Further studies indicated that the
brain changes were correlated with changes
in the rat's ability to solve problems.

Bronfenbrenner (1972), in his critique of studies conducted on maternal deprivation in humans, comes to these conclusions regarding the effects on emotional
and cognitive development. First, not all
infants in institutions suffer permanent
damage from maternal separation; only
those who do not have an emotionally satisfying relationship with a mother-figure

are affected. Second, maternal separation
before the age of six months is more det-
rimental than separation in the second
half of the first year, assuming there is
no emotionally satisfying experience with
a mother-figure. Third,

> although the joint effects of stimu-
> lus restriction and frustration of
> dependency drive are more debilitat-
> ing than those of stimulus restric-
> tion alone, they are more susceptible
> to recovery through subsequent inter-
> action with the environment, whereas
> the sequel of stimulus restriction in
> earliest infancy are more likely to
> persist into later life (pp. 289-90).

In summary, it can be said that perception is an active process involving
cortical participation. One perceives best
when stimulation is optimal, that is, when
it is neither too high nor too low.
Perceptual-cognitive development is facilitated by mother-infant interaction and
a child's overall competency is related to
the quality of maternal care.

7. STIMULATION IN INFANCY

Cecile C. Baker

> It appears that having a variety of
> things to listen to and to look at
> may be the most important for devel-
> opment during the first year of life.
> *Hunt (1964)*

The importance of stimulating experience during infancy has been stressed by
various theoretical orientations. Thompson
and Schaefer (1961) list several reasons
why experiences in early infancy have pervasive effects: (1) primacy--earlier experiences are more important than later
ones in the sense that they influence the
effects of a greater number of subsequent
events; (2) plasticity--functions that are
in the process of developing are more
amenable to change than functions that
have matured; (3) differentiation--events
occurring in infancy have a widespread ef-
efect due to the relative lack of differentiation of the infant; and (4) critical
periods in development--at certain periods

141

a wide range of stimuli is effective in altering behavioral development.

The idea of critical periods is also illustrated by Bloom (1964), who notes that the essential framework and basis for intellectual growth are firmly established by age four and that environmental effects are most influential during the periods of most rapid growth.

Learning theories give support to the fact that learnings that occur in infancy will be highly resistant to extinction because of the high probability of occurrence of variable interval and variable ratio reinforcement schedules (Moss 1967).

Piaget (1952) has implied that thinking does not merely emerge; it can be traced to the impact of experience upon functioning in the early months and years. His first stage in development, the sensorimotor period in which the infant becomes able to coordinate information from the various sensory modalities, extends from birth to two years, encompassing the period of infancy (Baldwin 1967).

Fowler (1969) has used the term "developmental learning" to refer to

> the cumulative effects of stimulation from all sources over the course of development. . . . Developmental learning is concerned with the process of how, over long time spans, stimulation develops the individual, piling up and transforming the organization of his knowlege and abilities (p. 158).

Probably the most influential theoretical framework in emphasizing the long-range consequences of infant experience is

psychoanalytic theory, which will serve as
the basis for this paper.

Bruner (1970) has listed five points
to be aware of in studying infant development theories such as those discussed
above.

1. While many theories tend to mini-
mize the importance of reciprocal relationships, influence exerted by the mother
figure is enormous.

2. While many theorists emphasize
stages in development, there is a gradual
but small acquisition of skill and competence on a day-to-day basis during infancy.

3. Affective factors contribute
greatly to cognitive development.

4. The child should be viewed as an
active participant, rather than recipient
of an enriched environment.

5. There should be continual, rather
than sporadic, intervention in infancy and
early childhood.

TYPES OF STIMULI

According to Freudian theory, stimuli
may be classified as either external or
instinctual. External stimuli are viewed
as dangerous energies from the outside
world that directly penetrate the infant
(Holt 1965). The stimulus barrier scales
down the intensity of these stimuli to a
level that the infant can manage

(Benjamin 1965). Instinctual stimuli originate within the infant as needs that may be satisfied by altering the internal source of stimulation (Holt 1965). In psychoanalytic theory, infant needs may also be seen as id drives that arouse the infant from homeostasis and promote activities to reduce the drive. As the infant learns which activities are most beneficial to drive reduction, patterns of behavior are established (White 1962).

Greenberg (1965) distinguished several types of stimuli: internal (stimuli from a source within the infant) and external (stimuli created by the mother and other agents); stimulation intended to restore quiescence and stimulation intended to maintain an existing balance in the infant; stimulation that is part of the gratification of a biological need (for example, hunger) and stimulation under other conditions (for example, play).

Yarrow (1968) classified stimuli as those that elicit or evoke responses, those that facilitate the expression of developmentally emergent behaviors, and those that support or maintain ongoing behavior patterns. Breckenridge and Murphy (1969) contend that strong stimuli that impel action have biological bases. As the individual adds experiences, these particular stimuli are modifed, although they essentially remain extensions of the individual's original stimuli. For a discussion of prenatal and birth experiences, see chapters 1 and 2.

STAGES OF NORMAL AUTISM

Stimulation during the stage of normal autism tends to have either an arousing or quieting effect, depending on the existing state of the infant (Moss 1967). The infant receives stimulation that raise tensions and create a general feeling of displeasure. As the tensions are lowered, he experiences pleasure. Sigmund Freud (1949) suggests that what is felt as pleasure or displeasure is not the absolute degree of the tensions but something in the rhythm of their changes.

Stimulations may be received by exteroceptors, which are receptor nerves sensitive to stimuli external to the organism, or by proprioceptors, which are sensitive to stimuli resulting primarily from actions of the body itself. Once received, stimuli activate particular sensory channels within the nervous system. The way in which receptor excitation is encoded and transmitted as nerve impulses to become reflex actions has been explained in detail by Spears and Hohle (1967).

The infant has a suppressive mechanism by which he is able to suppress disturbing reactions to stimuli that may be received while he is asleep. This same mechanism allows the infant to be put to sleep in the face of strong or disturbing stimuli. Apparently sleep may be the infant's way of shutting out disturbing stimuli so that he is capable of withstanding disturbances from the outside world (Brazelton 1969).

The stimulus barrier at this stage is a purely passive mechanism due to the

lack of neural maturation (Benjamin 1965).
This, coupled with the high perceptive
threshold of the infant (Spitz 1950),
causes him to react to both external and
instinctual (internal) stimulation with
diffuse (startle) reflexes (Schur 1960).
The infant does, not, however, differentiate his own tension-reducing attempts from
those of his mother. Research by Moss
(1967) indicates that during this stage
the behavior of the infant shapes the
mother's behavior.

Fenichel (1945) has related the concept of a passive stimulus barrier to the
infant's attempts to reduce tension in
this way:

> Innumerable stimuli pour out upon him
> which he cannot master. He is not in
> a position to move voluntarily. ...
> He knows no object world and has no
> ability yet to "bind" tension. ...
> Probably this being flooded by exci-
> tation is highly unpleasant and
> evokes the first mental tendency ...
> to get rid of the state of tension
> (p. 34)

When stimulated, stimulus-response
patterns may be set up, modified acord-
ding to the mother's style in infant-
mother interactions, and become conditioned as the pattern is repeated. In addition, the infant typically exhibits certain distinct reflex patterns (discussed
by Brazelton, 1969).

Reflex pattern	Produced by
Babinski reflex	stroking the sole of the foot

Reflex pattern	*Produced by*
grasping	stroking the palm of the hand
hand-to-mouth	stimulating the cheek or palm of the hand
Moro reflex	sudden change in position or sudden loud sound
righting	pulling the infant to a sitting position
rooting/ sucking	stimulating the mouth or snout region
tonic neck reflex	turning the head to the side

White (1959) has discussed responses to stimuli in terms of "effectance behavior," which he describes as a pattern of learning in which the infant activates, refines, and sharpens motor and perceptual skills through trying to cope with stimulation. Effectance, then, is the motivation that produces effects on the environment, or "what the sensori-neuro-muscular system wants to do when it is not occupied with homeostatic business" (White 1962, p. 216). The feeling of efficacy is that feeling that goes along with producing the above changes.

STAGE OF NORMAL SYMBIOSIS

During the stage of normal symbiosis the passive stimulus barrier disappears and an active stimulus barrier has not developed. The infant experiences an increase in overall sensitivity to external and internal stimulation and needs his mother to help in tension reduction to prevent his being overwhelmed by stimuli (Benjamin 1965, Mahler 1968).

Mother as Stimulus Barrier

As the mother assists the infant in regulating stimuli, each mother-infant pair evolves its own pattern of responses (Greenberg 1965). Benjamin (1965) hypothesized that failure on the part of the mother to meet the increased needs of the infant may be responsible for the reduction in effectiveness of the stimulus barrier and may be an important factor leading to a heightened predisposition to anxiety.

Maternal failure to provide for the reduction of excessive excitation may lead the infant to find his own outlet for tension reduction. Repetitive movements such as head-rocking and thumb-sucking induce soothing autostimulation, allowing the discharge of excitation and a return to homeostatic equilibrium. With excessive overstimulation, these motor responses are used increasingly and later may be used by the ego, especially for defense against overstimulation (Benjamin 1965, Greenberg 1965).

Greenberg notes:

Overstimulation in the form of excessive, intrusive, and overwhelming stimulation has been implicated as a precondition for later development of childhood schizophrenia, as an immediate factor in infantile feeding disorders, and as a disruptive influence upon established behavioral patterns (p. 853).

Too much handling and anxious stimulation at this time may also cause excessive crying and colic. Benjamin noted that
colic typically begins at three to four
weeks and disappears between two to four
months. Thus colic is present at the time
when the infant has neither an active or
passive stimulus barrier.

Additionally, overstimulation in infancy can result in stimulus hunger, which
is a condition where there are no satia-
tion experiences with respect to various
stimuli (Bellak 1963, Gediman 1971).
Bergman and Escalona (1949) found overstimulation to result in a lower stimulus
barrier.

On the basis of research on institutionalized infants, Brazelton (1969) concluded that too little stimulation inter-
feres with emotional growth and is thus
worse than too much stimulation. Greenberg
(1965) has contended that too little
stimulation, like overstimulation, can
lead to such motor responses as body rocking. Understimulation also causes lower
stimulus thresholds to develop and thus
predisposes the infant to disruption under
normal stimulus conditions. Brody (1956)
hypothesized that the frequency and/or intensity of nonnutritive sucking are correlated more positively with low environmental stimulation between three to six
months and less positively with low stimulation before three months and after six
months.

Active Stimulus Barrier

At eight to ten weeks the active stimulus barrier develops, and the infant is able to shut out stimuli without total dependence on the mother (Benjamin 1965). The infant begins to turn his attention toward the outer world, although primarily to things that are closely related to the mother. Schaffer and Emerson (1964) have suggested that the infant's need for the proximity of other people is not primary but arises from his need for stimulation in general. Although the other person's proximity is initially sought as only one source of stimulation among many, it will eventually be required in its own right.

One of the most prominent characteristics of the infant is his searching the environment for stimulation. By three months his responsiveness is well developed, and he actively seeks for arousing properties of his surroundings. He begins to explore through his sensorimotor abilities. These sensorimotor functions have three uses: (1) they satisfy needs; (2) they produce activity that forms thresholds levels that permit more efficient adaptive functioning; and (3) they pacify and soothe the infant by reducing his arousal level (Greenberg 1965).

The sense of vision is employed in visually directed reaching, visual exploration, visual accommodation, and the blink response (White 1967). A visual pattern develops which consists of turning to an outside stimulus and then back to the mother, especially to her face. That infants generally prefer face-like stimuli has been demonstrated by Fantz (1963, 1965). Spitz (1957) has contended that through the use of vision the infant begins to indicate choice by his head movements. "No" is indicated by a direct turning of the head to the side to dispose of the undesirable stimulus object by removing it from the visual field. "Yes" is indicated by an up and down movement of the head which allows the object to remain in the visual field and be reaffirmed.

The sense of touch is important in the development of a tactile communication system (Frank 1966). The infant experiences the soothing aspect of touch as well as the effect of firm, steady pressure. Freedom from tensions in the mother contributes much to the well-being of the infant (Greenacre 1960). Touch is also important in the beginning of object relations, in determining the self from the non-self. Touch and vision help the infant to distinguish himself from his mother. The infant begins to experience separateness from her through temporary loss of contact or through the experiencing of strong own-body sensations, different from sensations that have been experienced in contact with the mother. The fluctuation between oneness with the mother and separateness from her furnishes the beginning of what will also become a psychological separation (Greenacre 1960).

STAGE OF OBJECT RELATIONS

The development of object relations has been described by Winnicott (1960) as a phase of "living with," which implies the perception of objects as external to the self. The appearance in the external

world of objects that are the sources of
tension reduction of internal stimuli offers powerful stimulation for the development of the ego (Call 1964).

The growing maturational separateness
between infant and mother can be observed
by the end of the first six months in the
appearance of actively asserted pressure
against the mother. This pressure takes
on rhythmic qualities such as in jumping
up and down or playing peek-a-boo. The
mother can stimulate the development of
object realtions by engaging in similar
games with the infant. When the mother is
absent, the infant engages in bodily self-
stimulation, providing the kind of bodily
sensations that the mother provided for
him in moments of pleasurable interaction
(Escalona 1963).

The stimulus barrier becomes an ego
function; when bombarded by stimuli, the
infant reacts with either sensitization
(lowering of thresholds) or adaptation
(raising of thresholds) (Gediman 1971).
Indications of displeasure (anxiety) can
be distinguished in terms of avoidance behavior, and anticipations of pleasure can
be distinguished in the form of approach
behavior (Call 1964).

RESEARCH ON INFANT STIMULATION

Denenberg (1969) reviewed many animal
studies on infant stimulation and derived
from them principles that may also apply
to humans:

1. "Behaviors which have fundamental
adaptive evolutionary meaning to the ani-

mal are amenable to drastic modifications
by the appropriate manipulations of an
animal's experiences during early development" (p. 37).

2. The effexts of early experience
have long-term consequences; "this is not
a simple transitory phenomenon, but . . .
a very robust effect which can modify an
animal's behavior for its complete life-
time" (p. 38).

3. "Differential early experiences
are a significant cause of individual differences among animals" (p. 40).

4. "Stimulation in early life affects
a multiplicity of biological and behavioral processes" (p. 41).

5. "The age at which stimulation is
administered in infancy is extremely crucial" (p. 41).

In connection with the last point,
Denenberg noted that preweaning stimulation has a relatively greater impact upon
affective than cognitive processes in animals, whereas postweaning stimulation
plays the opposite role. He suspects that
preweaning stimulation, or handling in the
rat, is represented in the human during
the first four to twenty-four weeks of
life, and concludes that the use of an enriched environment in humans should begin
at approximately six months.

From a similar review of animal studies, Greenberg (1965) concluded that mild
or moderate stimulation during the early
weeks of life raises the animal's thresholds and increases its ability to handle

stimulus loads. This beneficial effect is
illustrated in behavior that shows less
emotionality, better resistance to stress,
and more social and exploratory behavior
with greater motivation.

Levine et al. (1967) reported that
handled rats were more active and defe-
cated less than unhandled rats. They concluded that stimulation in infancy results
in an animal which is less responsive to
novel stimuli; that is, is less emotional.

Morton et al. (1963) found that the
onset of estrus occurred significantly
earlier for female rats which were handled
in infancy and group reared after weaning.
Male rats which had been handled were
found to have heavier prostates and semi-
nal vesicles than unhandled males.

Results of research on premature human infants who were stroked five minutes
per hour for the first ten days of life
showed that these infants were more active, regained initial birth weights
faster, and were described as physically
healthier in terms of growth and motor development than were premature infants who
had not been stimulated (Solkoff et al.
1969).

Landauer and Whiting (1964), in a
study of eighty societies, found that in
those societies where infant males were
pierced or molded in some manner the adult
males were over two inches taller than in
comparable societies that did not engage
in the practices. The fact that the increase in height was the same whether one
or both of the stressful practices occurred suggests a threshold effect where
any sufficient stress will produce maximum
effect. The authors suggest that the first
two years of life may be a critical period

for the effect of stress.

In a similar study, Whiting et al. (1968), holding parental stature constant, found the adult stature of individuals who had been inoculated before two years to be significantly greater than that of individuals not inoculated. Although the study did not control for race and diet, a growth-accelerating influence of early physiological stress was concluded.

RESEARCH ON INFANT DEPRIVATION

Goldfarb (1945) summarized the typical family experience of the infant as one in which a loving parent person, with whom a reciprocal relationship develops, provides continuous contact that is a source of constant stimulation. In reviewing studies of infants in institutions, Brody (1956) found that they have a quite atypical early environment.

> The classic picture of the institutionalized infant is one of impoverishment, which in past times referred to physical needs and now refers more to the need for psychic stimulation. The institutionalized infant suffers from a lack of opportunity to practice most acts that seem to be necessary for adequate maturation of ego functions (pp. 100-101).

Research on infants in institutions has, indeed, found that such infants experience a lag in mental growth which is maintained even under new conditions of enriched stimulation (Goldfarb 1945). In

addition, they have a dominately passive
personality which is not able to assimi-
late new sources of stimulation and new
relationships (Goldfarb 1945); tend toward
delinquent character development (Bowlby
1944); and respond to many stimuli with
anxiety (Spitz 1950).

APPLICATION OF KNOWLEDGE
ABOUT INFANT STIMULATION

The importance of stimulation in infancy has been recognized for many years.
In 1914 Stoner wrote of her experiences
with her infant daughter, "I tried never
to excite unduly the child's nervous system, yet not to leave her in such uninter-
esting surroundings that she would be com-
pelled to such her thumb for amusement"
(p. 26). More recently, Fowler (1962,
1968) reviewed studies of people with high
abilities and concluded, "In no instance
(where documentation exists) have I found
any individual of high ability who did not
experience intensive early stimulation as
a central component of his development"
(1968, p. 17).

The widespread recognition that
stimulation in infancy is important for
later development has led to the establishment of infant stimulation programs.
Among these programs are those established
by Caldwell and Richmond (1968), Gordon
(1971), Weikart and Lambie (1968) and
Strickland (1971).

A primary focus of most infant stimulation programs is that the mother learn
how to stimulate her infant in her own way

without prolonged interference from an outside agent. The best way for a mother to begin to feel secure in doing this is to understand basic principles underlying infant stimulation:

1. Play and games must be adaptable to the needs of individual infants and mother-infant pairs rather than stereotyped activities to be reproduced according to specific instructions.

2. The mother should not mechanically engage in activities but should relate and react to the human element in her baby. Many mothers, especially lower-class ones, need to be taught this distinction.

3. In order to play, an infant must be capable of attention and discrimination, have control over that part of the body involved in play, and must be in the presence of a reciprocating party (Call 1968).

4. A necessary condition for the development of a game is familiarity with the routine of an environment.

5. Immediately after feeding is a good time for games, as infants are quiet and alert for a short period of time.

6. Stimulation should occur between feedings as well as immediately before, during, and after.

7. Most games occur on the mother's lap. Her hands provide objects to assist in the development of object relations (Call 1968).

8. Parental reciprocation in and contribution to play help the infant to distinguish between human and nonhuman objects.

9. Peek-a-boo provides practice in
separating the self from someone else and
experiencing reunion. It also allows the
infant to practice his ability to make the
mother reappear and his ability to make
himself withdraw (Schur 1960).

10. During the stage of normal symbiosis, the infant feels omnipotent and
believes that he can make things appear
and disappear by closing his eyes, moving
his head, etc. The infant should be allowed to experience a manageable amount of
frustration so that he comes to know the
limitation of reality rather than the
feeling of omnipotence.

11. An infant responds to objects that
are within a particular range of sensory
values and which are appropriate to his
stage of development.

12. Play and games should involve as
many sensorimotor functions as possible in
order that the resultant anchorage to an
object is determined by many interrelated
functions (holding, rooting, hand-mouth
system, vision, etc.) (Call 1968).

13. In new situations the infant needs
to readjust his regulatory mechanisms.
Tense handling at these times in order to
"shut him up" may overstimulate him and
increase the crying. He may have been crying to let off his own tension and is then
forced to handle the adult's tensions as

well as his own (Brazelton 1969).

14. If the mother understands her infant's particular style, she can stimulate
him accordingly. If she also understands
normal infant development, she can assess
his progress.

15. Behavioral integration during infancy is dependent on neural development.
Both are dependent on the early sensory
environment (Greenberg 1965).

SUMMARY

Fiske and Maddi (1961) have offered
eight propositions regarding stimulation
which aptly summarize the content and implications of this paper.

1. The impact of a stimulus is its
momentary contribution to the activation level of an organism [p. 18].

2. An organism's level of activation
varies directly over time with the
total impact of current stimulation
[p. 19].

3. The impact of a stimulus is derived not only from the intensity and
meaningfulness of the stimulus but
also from the extent to which it provides variation from prior stimulation [p. 23].

4. For any task, there is a level of
activation which is necessary for
maximally effective performance [p.

31].

5. The behavior of an organism tends to modify its activation level toward the optimal zone for the task at hand [p. 35].

6. For each stage in an organism's sleepwakefulness cycle, there is a characteristic or normal level of activation [p. 38.].

7. In the absence of specific tasks, the behavior of an organism is directed toward the maintenance of activation at the characteristic or normal level [p. 42].

8. Negative affect is ordinarily experienced when activation level differs markedly from normal level; positive affect is associated with shifts of activation toward normal level [p. 46.]

Principles such as these, coupled with theoretical explanations, contribute to understanding the need for and the effects of stimulation on the infant. Research, however, is just beginning to establish concrete findings regarding the lasting effects of infant stimulation or the lack of it. Much more knowledge is needed in this area before an understanding of the components of optimum infant stimulation can be established and disseminated to the general public.

8. PERCEPTUAL-COGNITIVE DEVELOPMENT

IN INFANCY

Julinda Abu Nasr

We do not just see, we look;
We do not just hear, we listen.
Gibson (1969)

Many authors agree that one of the
most widely studied areas in the field of
developmental psychology in the last decade has been human infancy. Evidence
gained from research seems to suggest that
infancy is probably a "critical developmental period" for a variety of major processes including motivation, intelligence,
language, social, emotion, perceptual, and
cognitive development. White (1971), among
others, agrees that there is a great need
for longitudinal studies in the field like
those of Bayley, Gesell, McGraw, Piaget,
White, Fels Institute Studies and so on.
This knowlege is necessary for the formulation of a comprehensive theory of development. Most commonly, individual researchers have studied isolated phenomena.

One such area has been cognition, or the study of the mental processes of the individual.

Cognitive development is definitely linked to perceptual development. To be able to understand how the infant constructs reality, we need to know something about the nature of the information available to him. This information is related to him through his perceptual structure, or sensory schema, which is present at birth. Thus, in studying perception we get some insight into the interaction of the organism with its environment.

This process of interaction is achieved through the discriminatory and selective function of the organism. The organism extracts information that is relevant to its development. What is learned may elicit direct response, or it may be stored for future use, or both. In either case new mental structures of schemas develop which in turn alter the way in which the child will perceive and respond to its environment.

This differentiation and discrimination is a function of repeated examination of stimuli through experience and practice. The intake of information gradually becomes more efficient through past experience. This in turn helps in the process of integration and adaptation of the stimulus input that is necessary for knowledge acquisition (Bartley 1969, Brackbill 1958, Gibson 1969, Piaget 1952, Watson 1966, White 1971).

The human infant is born with a diversified reflex repertoire. He begins immediately to interact with the postnatal environment. His neuromuscular growth is rapid and complex, so his abilities devel-

op at a fast rate and one can see a re-
markable change in the first few months of
life. Because this growth is so rapid, it
is difficult to distinguish between contributions made by maturation or neurological growth and those made by experience. Behavioral scientists have proposed
some explanations based on the scant
knowledge that is available mainly from
animal studies and limited human studies.
However, the evidence available seems to
ascertain that a certain amount of stimulation from the environment is necessary
for the healthy development of the organism.

The role of stimulation in development has been discussed by a number of
authors among whom are Deutsch (1964),
Fowler (1962), Gordon (1971), Hebb (1949),
and Hunt (1961). Other pertinent issues
that have occupied the literature on this
subject are the manner of its development,
the theoretical framework to explain its
implications, the optimal age to introduce
it, and the style of presenting it. It is
not within the scope of this chapter to
deal with the above issues; nevertheless,
a brief mention will be made in relation
to tactile, auditory, visual stimulation,
and the consequent adverse effects of deprivation on development. However, the major concern of this presentation is visual
perception.

It has been reported that babies are
highly responsive to touch. The psychoanalytic writers have stressed the importance
of tactile stimulation in early life for
normal development. Anna Freud has asserted that there is a relationship between early tactile stimulation and later
disturbance. This has been confirmed by a

number of animal studies that have indicated some kind of emotional problems in
cases of tactile deprivation. There is
some evidence that schizophrenia might be
related to perceptual deprivation. Monkeys
experiencing isolation and minimum tactile
stimulation had biochemical abnormalities
that were similar to those of some human
schizophrenics (Casler 1968, Denenberg
1967, Harlow 1958, Scott 1968).

The data from studies on neglected
babies, or those given minimum care, support the hypothesis that deprivation slows
down the rate of development and in some
cases leads to regression. More specifically, Dennis (1957, 1960) has asserted
that these children might have long delays
in learning certain skills such as sitting
and walking.

This problem was first approached by
the emotional climate provided by the
mother, but new knowledge has been derived
from a number of animal studies. It has
confirmed the fact that tacticle stimulation is important for the normal development of the nervous and neuroendocrine
systems as well as for the development of
behavioral capacities. It has also indicated that the presence or absence of
physical stimulation is more important
than the manner in which it is given.

In support of this issue, Casler
(1968) has reported higher mean scores on
the Gesell Developmental Scale for eight
infants who were given twenty minutes of
tactile stimulation daily for a period of
ten weeks. The fact that the assistants
were trained to be impersonal in their
handling did not seem to affect the process of development. Motor ability was the
only function that was not influenced by

extra handling. Lack of auditory stimulation as well as lack of tactile stimulation seemed to constitute a further handicap.

With the exception of tactile stimulation, visual stimulation may be the most influential source of early experience. Studies by Riesen (1961) on monkeys and kittens have shown that structural as well as functional development is hampered by visual deprivation. Chimpanzees that were reared in darkness and tested at different stages in their development suffered from poor vision due to the deterioration and loss of ganglion cells. Hubel and Wiesel (1963) report similar results on work done with kittens who had one eye closed by suture from birth to the age of three months.

One may conclude from these data that there might be a critical period in visual-cognitive development early in life after the ears and eyes first become functional.

These are but a few of the studies on stimulation deprivation, a topic that has led to interest in detecting perceptual abilities early in life and in learning more about the role they play in development. Increased interest in the vision of newborns is demonstrated by the growing amount of research in visual perception. Visual acuity, form discrimination, visual preference, rate and sequence of development, stimulus input and its effect on development, and other controlled visual behavior are among the issues that are getting a great deal of the researcher's attention. However, one can see a tipped balance in favor of the neonate and some neglect of the older infant. White (1971) claims that a large percentage of the studies are on neonates under four days of age, because of the availability of these babies in hospitals and the low expense involved in studying them there as opposed to studying them at home.

It is interesting to note the variety of instruments and methods used in studying this area of perception. It is agreed that one of the most thorough methods is the naturalistic method of observation, which has been used in longitudinal studies like those of Gesell, McGraw, Piaget, White, and others. Behavior is observed in natural settings and recorded and analyzed by competent observers.

Experimental cross-sectional studies have also been done by a larger number of researchers. The instruments used included a variety of devices, some of which are patterns of human faces regular or scrambled, geometric figures, blank shapes, bright panels, colored disks, rotating disks, and optical illusions. Fixation has been generally used as an index of visual awareness and in some cases of visual preference. Responses such as the startle reflex, the surprise response, the smiling response, the blinking response, the head movement, and the heart rate activity have also been used as indices of visual awareness. Procedures involving stimulus preference and operant conditioning have been used to study the infant's ability to perceive.

With advanced technology, highly elaborate technical devices have been developed to record behavior: cardiograms to measure deceleration and acceleration of cardiac activity, electrodes to measure eyeblink responses, retinoscopes to measure fixation time, and a host of other mechanical, magnetic, and polygraphic devices that are described by the different researchers, who include Bower (1971), Brackbill (1958), Fantz (1967), Gibson (1969), Kagan (1966), Kessen (1967), Pick (1970), White (1971), and others.

Gibson and Walk (1960) have used the "visual cliff" in studying depth perception. This consists of a deep box covered with a large sheet of plate glass. A patterned surface is visible under the glass; half of it is placed directly under the glass, while the other half drops sharply down several feet and continues across the bottom half of the box. The baby placed in the center gets the impression that he is standing or crawling on the edge of a cliff.

In the following section, a brief survey of the research in the field of perceptual-cognitive development will be reported.

REVIEW OF SOME RESEARCH STUDIES

White (1971) has remarked that the first month of life is a poor time to study visual-motor functions because the infant is only alert 5 percent of the time; the rest of the time he is drowsy or sleepy. Infants are not capable of any but the most primitive visual functions, and they do not seem to engage in visual inquiry activities. There is great difference in the quality of gazing between the neonate and the three-month-old infant.

Fantz (1963), on the other hand, who represents the more nativistic position,

sees the newborn infant as considerably
more able in the visual modality than
White does. In one study, out of eighteen
infants under five days of age, eleven
looked longest at a schematic face pattern, five at a bull's eye pattern and two
at a section of newsprint. The infant's
performance was consistent in pattern
preference in all test situations, which
led Fantz to conclude that there is an unlearned ability for form preference.

In an earlier study, Fantz (1961)
observed forty-nine infants whose ages
ranged from four days to six months. They
were shown targets the size and shape of
the human head. One was a real human face,
another a scrambled face, and the third a
solid black area. The real face was fixated most, the scrambled next, and the
black area last. Fantz concluded that in
the human infant there is an unlearned,
primitive meaning in the form perception.

This finding was challenged by Kagan
et al. (1966) because of using fixation as
an index of visual preference. Thirty-four
four-month-old babies were exposed to four
different three-dimensional representations of human faces--a regular face, a
scrambled face, a face without eyes, and a
blank face. Fixation times to the regular
scrambled faces were the same, but significant differences were reported in
smiling and cardiac responses. The researchers concluded that fixation used
alone as an index for perception might be
misleading.

Thomas (1965) had different results
from his two-week-old infants. He reported
that they fixated the checkerboard more
than they did a schematic oval drawing of
a face. This was confirmed by Hershenson

(1965), who reported lack of consistency in fixation of the human face in the neonate.

One can see that the results are contradictory; however, supporting evidence of the interest of the infant in the human face is prevelant in the reaearch on older infants.

McCall and Kagan (1967) reported a study on ninety-four four-month-old infants who were presented slides of achromatic regular and irregular faces and random shapes. The human face elicited a longer cardiac deceleration. The authors suggested that four-month-old infants are attracted more by the human face, a form that is familiar, than they are to unfamiliar objects.

Gibson (1969) summarized the results of infants' reactions between the ages of two to seven months to the human face. All the studies reported revealed some awareness, and in some cases preference, to the human face. One may conclude from this evidence that the familiarity and probably the meaning of the human face to the older infant are important factors in perception.

Another preference that has been noted in the neonate is that for simple and linear patterns as opposed to complex patterns. The controversy on this issue is apparent in the writings of a number of authors among whom are Kagan, Kessen, Hershenson, Thomas, and Watson.

Hershenson (1964) found that brightness was an important variable in pattern preference. Newborns reacted more favorably to medium brightness than they did to dim or bright lights. Kagan et al. (1966) reported that the contour of the stimulus

seemed to determine the fixation time of
their thirty-six four-month-old infants
rather than the complexity of the pattern.
Kessen (1967) stressed the point that more
knowledge of the specific response of the
newborn to a single figure rather than the
general direction of the infant's ocular
orientation is necessary for interpreting
research results. Watson (1966) has contended that infants are sensitive to object orientation, which is another variable that might interfere in preference
results. The capacity to perceive orientation is well established by fourteen
weeks.

All the above evidence points to the
fact that precaution has to be taken in
interpreting results. Hershenson's study
in which he used a simple checkerboard
and a complex checkerboard offers support
to the possibility that newborns prefer
the simple pattern, since they fixated
longer on the simple pattern, Hershenson
et al. (1965) also found that the newborn
fixated longer on random shapes of ten independent turns drawings than they did on
random shapes with twenty turns. The study
reported earlier by Thomas offered similar
results.

Fantz and Nevis (1967) studied two-
week-old infants who were presented with
a variety of black and white patterns
and a plain gray square. They reported
that all the babies indicated significant
preference for the simple linear arrange-
ment. Similar findings were reported by
the same author in 1958 and were confirmed
in a more recent study in 1962 where black
line segments in four different arrange-
ments were presented to forty-nine infants
between the ages of one to fourteen

months. The results supported the preference for linear and simple patterns in the
one-month-old infant. However, a significant change from linear to circular patterns was observed in the second month.
This shift in preference was explained by
the maturity of the oculomotor system during the second month (Fantz & Nevis 1967).

Scott (1968) maintained that there is
some transition that takes place in visual
capacities about that time of the child's
life. He went on to explain that the alpha
waves in the human electrocephalogram,
which are associated with visual attention
in the adult and are almost entirely absent at birth, make their appearance in
the second month. They become well established by four months. Because of this
oculomotor coordination the organism is
capable of processing more complex information, thus explaining the superiority of
the older infant to the neonate in handling complex stimuli.

This change overlaps with the process
of socialization, and it is closely related to the ability of the child to discriminate faces and other objects. This is
also the time that infants begin to smile
and show alert and exploratory behavior as
well as an increased interest in their environment in general and in their hands in
particular. Responses to nearby objects
reveal accommodation and convergence of
visual abilities which might lead one to
consider this period as the beginning of
voluntary action (White 1971).

During the next period, which is from
three and a half to six months, the infant
begins to observe his own hands and spends
hundreds of hours studying them tactually
and visually. White refers to this period

as the "visually directed period." Until
this point in his development, objects
have no conceptual value for the infant;
but now the fact that he can fixate on,
reach for, and grasp an object gives the
infant a different meaning of his environment. Piaget (1952) refers to this stage
of development as the preparatory stage
for the emergence of awareness of an object world that has an independent existence from that of the child. White describes this awareness in the following
fashion. "Things grasped are now looked
at, things in the mouth are now touched,
things heard are now looked at" (1971, p.
87) all of which suggests coordination and
unity in the perceptual system.

Depth perception is another area that
has motivated interest in research. Infants at the onset of crawling were tested
using the visual cliff described earlier
in this chapter. The results seem to indicate that the infant at six months has
some awareness of depth. Walk and Gibson
(1961) found that 90 percent of the infants at all ages (six and a half to fifteen months) who responded in the cliff
situation did avoid the deep side. However, since the test depended upon the infant's ability to move, it is difficult to
know when the infant starts perceiving
depth. Bower (1964), using operant conditioning in his study, claimed that infants
as young as one month appear to discriminate some of the cues that specify depth.
Perception of the property of solidity in
the object has been studied by Bower
(1971) through methods of visual illusions. He maintained that infants as young
as two weeks exhibited awareness of an approaching object and expected the seen ob-

ject to have tactile consequences. These results were drawn from the fact that the infants withdrew at the sigh of an approaching object.

From his studies of perception of objects by sixteen-week-old infants, Bower concluded that younger infants are not affected by feature differences of the object "but respond to a change in motion but not to a change in size, shape or color. They ignore features to such an extent that I would suggest they respond not to moving objects but to movements" (p. 37). He suggested that for older infants objects have permanent features, while to the infant of sixteen weeks and younger an object becomes a different object every time it moves to a new location. It might be premature at this point to be so sure about these results, but the author contends that more research in this area is under way.

Color preference was another area that motivated interest in researchers. Spears (1964) studied color preference in four-month-old infants. Fixation time was used as an index of preference. He found a preference ordering of blue, red, yellow, gray with only the preference of blue over gray statistically significant. The research in this area is still scant however; so it is difficult to infer any results from it.

Very little research has been done on auditory perception. The problem is well stated by Eisenberg, who remarked that auditory research is a vast wasteland and that there is a great need to know more about the learning that takes place between six and eighteen months (White 1971).

There is some evidence that auditory receptors can be stimulated in the womb. Distinct responses of the fetus in the womb were elicited by striking the bathtub in which the mother was seated. A wide variety of tones was used to stimulate the child in utero by different investigators (Bartley 1969).

Eisenberg (1969) has indicated that neonates give differential responses to different auditory stimuli indicating that they can differentiate sounds. Both Scott (1968) and Steinschneider et al. (1966) have found that the threshold of neonates two to five days old was less than 70 db, using changes in heart beat as an index of sensitivity. On the ability of the six-month-old, Friedlander (1970) has stated that it is probable that he can hear well enough to discriminate words and inflections.

Olfactory perception is another area that has been poorly studied. The few studies reported were on the neonate (Engen et al. 1963).

EARLY EXPERIENCES AND PERCEPTION

The interaction relation between heredity and environment is a controversial issue between nativists and empiricists. However, in some cases mild or enriching manipulations have been undertaken with children. Of course, this procedure has been used mostly with animals, and the literature is abundant with it. The enrichment technique investigation of perceptual effects of early experience has not been widely used with human subjects.

White (1971) has enriched the environment of institutionalized infants by providing extra handling for a group of children twenty minutes a day. Vestibular stimulation in the form of stabiles over the crib, pacifiers mounted on the crib rails, and colored striped mittens worn on the babies' hands were used. Data were gathered on a number of developmental areas including visual attention, visually directed reaching, visual accomodation, hand regard, and Gesell tests.

The results indicated important functional relationships between rearing conditions and the developmental process. The accelerated rate of development in the experimental group was significant, suggesting that enrichment modifications might alter the coordination as well as the rate of development of schemas in the infant.

These results were also achieved by Greenberg et al. (1968), who found that acceleration of the blink response to changes in visible stimulation was a consequence of continuous exposure to objects provided through stabiles over the infants from the sixth to the fourteenth week of life. The blink response came in the eighth week in the experimental group as opposed to eleven weeks in the control group.

Kagan (1965) and Sigelman (1969) have offered evidence that the reflective child has prolonged visual attention. Watson (1971), on the basis of his studies and from evidence in the literature in cognitive-perceptual development, concluded that the possibility exists that differences in "cognitive style" may originate in early "attention experiences."

SUMMARY

All the evidence presented in this brief survey of the wide field of perceptual-cognitive development indicates the need for a wider scope of knowledge to understand this complex being known as the human infant. It is true that new devices in studying behavior are used, that highly technical equipment is developed, that a lot of work is being done; but there is still a long way to go. It is difficult at this point of our knowledge of perception and cognition to draw any definite conclusions. The controversey that is prevalent among researchers is apparent in the literature. However, one can observe some trends that are pointing in certain directions. These are a few of the assumptions that were made by the different authors studied:

1. Newborns are capable of far more differential visual functions than previously believed.

2. Infants are attracted to patterns.

3. There is a definite preference for simple and linear patterns in the newborn.

4. Older infants--from four months on--prefer more complex patterns.

5. Older infants prefer familiar patterns.

6. Infants perceive depth, shape, size, color, and space.

7. Infants perceive movement rather than objects moving.

8. Brightness is an important variable in perception.

9. There is a sequential pattern in perceptual development.

10. The rate of perceptual development may be hastened by enriching stimulation.

11. The rate of perceptual development may be hampered by deprivation of stimulation.

12. There is a relationship between the infant's visual response and cognitive style.

To summarize, we can say that present research is pointing in this direction: that there is a specific pattern of perceptual-cognitive development and that this pattern may be altered by manipulating the early environment. This may be achieved either in the form of sensory deprivation and restriction or in the form of enrichment and enhancement of stimulation. Our main concern is to determine how these changes affect the growing and maturing organism in the process of development.

9. MOTHER-INFANT INTERACTION IN

PERCEPTUAL-COGNITIVE DEVELOPMENT

Moon-Hi Ro

> Babies grasp the world with their
> eyes and then with their hands. Vis-
> ion is therefore a prime constituent
> in the development of the total
> child.
>
> *Gesell (1950)*

The study of the intellectual development of children invariably evokes the
name Jean Piaget, who has given us more
information in this area than anyone else.
He defines infancy as a sensorimotor stage
and views sensorimotor intelligence in
terms of actions (Piaget 1952). Thus, in
infancy, modification of the infant's reflexes, such as sucking and grasping,
takes place through experiences; and the
infant accommodates and assimilates these
new experiences into his repertoire of responses.

Hebb (1949), theorizing on the neuro-

physiological basis of intellectual
growth, concluded that experience is an
essential mediator of neural connections
and a requirement for the formation of
cell assemblies. These neural assemblies
become relatively fixed functional units
(autonomous central processes), whose sequence and phasing in the associative cortex can be formed only by receptor in-
puts--that is, by sensory experience.
Hunt (1964) built his conception of learning and intelligence on the basis of
Hebb's work. According to Hunt, the earliest experience or primary learning forms
much of the pattern for later information
processing. In this primary learning, the
mother is seen as the mediator of the
child's environment.

Infants are not only capable of considerable early learning, but also can
adapt and modify their behavior to the environment (Horowitz 1968, White 1971). Research has documented individual differences of development during infancy, indicating that the manner in which a baby experiences his environment can affect not
only affectional but also cognitive development. Yarrow, et al. (1972) noted that
the cognitive motivational behaviors in
infants are particularly related to the
social environment. Schaefer (1972), in
reviewing evidence on the use of parents
as educators of young childre, emphasized
particularly that the nature of parent-
child interaction is the crucial factor
which influences the child's cognitive
functioning.

Escalona (1968) found that frequent
maternal contact with the baby and a highly stimulating home environment were associated with accelerated intellectual de-

velopment. On the other hand, Wachs et al. (1971) reported that "over-stimulating" homes, particularly in regard to noise level and activity, produced infants with the poorest cognitive development. Thus, it is assumed that stimulation is not a unitary dimension. Cognitive development is influenced by mutual feedback and adaptation during the interactions of the mother-infant pair.

SOCIAL CLASS

Since social class membership reflects different living conditions, it has been a convenient dimension on which to compare mother-infant interaction. While some studies have failed to show social class differences in intellectual performance in infants (Bayley 1965, Golden and Birns 1968), others have revealed significant social class differences in mother-infant interaction and cognitive growth in infants.

Tulkin and Kagan (1972), studying the first-born ten-month-old infant girls from middle- and lower-class Caucasian families, found social class differences in mother-infant interaction. Infants were seen for two, two-hour home observations, which were conducted when they were awake and not being fed or diapered. Mother-infant interaction was also scored for one laboratory session.

The results showed significant social class differences in home milieu and in infant and mother behaviors. Mothers in the lower-class homes watched more television; there were more people interacting

with the infants; and the infants had fewer objects to play with and spent less
time in free exploration. Although there
were no class differences in crying or
fretting, middle-class infants vocalized
more, crawled more often, and played more
often. Maternal behaviors, however,
yielded the most important findings. Compared to lower-class mothers, middle-class
mothers had more positive interactions
with their infants, gave their babies more
objects to play with, showed them pictures
and played peek-a-boo, and soothed their
babies more following fretting or prohibitions. The primary difference was in maternal verbal behavior; middle-class
mothers talked more to their babies, both
spontaneously and in response to their infants' vocalizations.

These differences are particularly
significant because they are correlated
with the mothers' beliefs about how early
an infant learns and communicates. Lower-
class mothers less frequently believed
that their infants were capable of learning and communicating with other people.
Thus they felt it was unnecessary to make
attempts for verbal interaction with their
infants.

Lewis and Wilson (1972), in a study
concerned with interaction between twelve-
week-old infants and their mothers, also
found striking differences in mother-
infant interaction as a function of social class. They observed social class
differences in four dimensions: attachment, stimulation, reinforcement, and
style of response. In general, lower-class
mothers showed more behaviors strengthening the attachment bond, such as more
smiling and holding. Moreover, lower-class

mothers provided almost the same amount of
stimulation and reinforcement for their
infants as middle-class mothers did. However, there was a different style of responding. Middle-class mothers vocalized
when their infants vocalized, whereas
lower-class mothers tended to touch their
infants when they vocalized. They also
touched, held, and smiled at the baby more
frequently than did the middle-class mothers. This resulted in more advanced visual
behavior in the lower-class infants.

Although the cognitive and attentive
data showed somewhat superior cognitive
functioning among infants from the lower-
class, middle-class infants vocalized more
than lower-class infants following maternal vocalization.

The lower-class infants' superior
performance in infancy was explained as a
result of the greater mother-infant proximal interaction, such as touching and
rocking. Lewis and Wilson, relying on
Sigel's (1970) distancing hypothesis, believe that while proximal interaction facilitated early prerepresentational
thought, distancing interaction such as
vocalization response facilitated the
ability to deal with higher cognitive
functioning (representational thought) after two years.

The evidence thus shows that social
class differences in mother-infant interactions do exist, especially in the area
of verbal behavior. The question is whether the style of maternal verbal response
truly affects the cognitive growth in infants. A study by Streissguth and Bee
(1972) provides some of the answers. They
attempted to find how a mother talks to
her baby when she tries to teach him some-

thing and how she structures a teaching
situation for the infant's problem solving.

They studied seventy-nine mother-
infant pairs from two different educational backgrounds of mothers and from infants
from ages nine to eighteen months in a
simple laboratory free-play situation followed by a teaching task, In both free-
play and teaching settings, the mother
held the infant on her lap at a table.
During free play, a variety of toys appropriate to a wide age range were available,
and the mother was instructed to let the
baby play freely with them. Following five
minutes of free play, the toys were removed, and a new task was presented which
the mother was asked to teach her child.
The tasks were such things as putting
three blocks in a cup for the nine-month-
olds and a simple form-board task for the
fifteen-month-olds.

The findings showed significant differences in the behavior of mothers in the
two situations. All mothers were much more
active with their infants in the teaching
situation than in free play, apparently
because they perceived the teaching situation as requiring more active intervention. The two groups of mothers, however,
differed significantly in their teaching
styles, particularly in their differential
use of feedback to the infant about his
performance. In free play, two groups of
mothers used about the same amount of
positive reinforcement (statement of approval and praise), but the lower-
education-group mothers used much more
negative reinforcement (state of disap-
proval and criticism). In the teaching
situation, both groups gave their infants

the same amount of overall feedback. However, the higher-education mothers used four times as much positive as negative reinforcement, while the lower-education mothers used almost the same amount of positive and negative reinforcement. Mothers with lower education also used more demonstrations in teaching and were generally more specific in the type of help and suggestions they gave their infants. Mothers with higher education used teaching strategies for maintaining the infant's attention and focusing him on the task but did not give as much specific instruction on how to solve the problem. These differences in feedback patterns and teaching strategies were found among mothers of infants of all ages studied.

Streissguth and Bee assumed that such differential reinforcement histories given by mothers from different social classes could be an influential consequence on the infant's later problem solving. In a similar study of interaction between mothers and children, Hess and Shipman (1965) showed the mother's teaching style to be a predictor of the child's later intellectual functioning and school performance, favoring the higher-education mother.

STIMULATION IN
PERCEPTUAL-COGNITIVE DEVELOPMENT

Many excellent studies suggest that certain types of stimulation may facilitate the fundamental sensorimotor acquisition. Researchers have been content to use the infant's visual activities--such as visual alertness, attentiveness, and visu-

al exploratory behavior--as indices of
cognitive function.

Korner and Grobstein (1966) identified a condition that influences visual
alertness. They found that picking up a
crying newborn and putting him to the
shoulder not only stopped crying but also
increased the frequency of eye openings,
alertness, and scanning. They suggested
that a change in the state of arousal,
which is under the mother's control, apparently evokes visual behavior.

The importance of tactual stimulation in the neonatal period was also found
in the study of Wachs and Cucinotta
(1971). They reported that the infants who
received early tactual stimulation through
140 minutes of supplementary experience
during the first three days of life showed
a significantly faster learning at four
days of age and greater visual attentiveness at 30 days of age. However they emphasized that periodic partial stimulation had little permanent effect on later
learning.

White (1967, 1969), who attempted the
first conventional study of sensorimotor
function in infants' visual exploratory
behavior, showed that extra handling
(tactual-vestibular stimulation) by a
caretaker during the first month of life
increased the visual attentiveness of institutionalized infants. He also found
that continuous motility stimulation and
visually enriched surroundings facilitated
visual-motor development during the first
half-year of life.

Goldberg (1972) reported, in the
study of the mother-infant interaction in
Zambia, that Zambian infants who were carried on their mothers' backs received

close visual and kinesthetic contact with
their mothers. This type of stimulation
resulted in outstanding intellectual development in Zambian infants. According to
Piaget's theory (1952), the stimulation
provided to Zambian infants was the ideal
means for learning cues relating to sucking and feeding. This suggests not only
the importance of sensori-motor stimulation during infancy, by the means of close
contact with the infant, but also the appropriateness of stimulation to behavior
capacities at a given level of maturation
for cognitive function.

There has also been an increased interest in viewing infant's vocalization as
cognitive functioning. Rheingold et al.
(1959) increased vocalizations of three-
month-old institutionalized infants by
presenting multisensory stimulation for
two days. On the other hand, Robson (1967)
has emphasized the developmental significance of eye-to-eye contact between mothr
and infant during the first six months of
life. According to Robson, eye-to-eye contact can focus and hold the infant's attention more successfully than many other
internal and external perceptual events.
The study by Kagan (1969) supports
Robson's thesis. Kagan found that vocalization and fixation time to human faces
or voices was more stable for girls between eight and thirteen months than for
boys. He noted that mothers who were motivated to accelerate their daughters' mental development were likely to spend a lot
of time in face-to-face vocalization with
them.

Tulkin (1973) investigated the reactions of forty-six ten-month-old first
born white female infants from both

middle-class and lower-class families to
the tape-recordings of their mothers'
voice and a stranger's voice. He found
that the middle-class infant vocalized and
looked more at his mother after hearing
his mother's voice and more at the coder
after the stranger's voice than did infants from the lower class. Tulkin sees
this greater differential in reactions of
middle-class infants to auditory stimuli
as the result of the infants' experiences
with more verbal stimulations from their
mothers in the home.

Another significant factor in increasing the infants' vocalization was
the contingency of social reward to the
infant's vocalization (Weisberg 1963). The
effect of this contingency of social reward to the infant's vocalization was also
found in Wahler's longitudinal investigation (1969) of social development of a
single infant from three to thirty-one
weeks of age. He reported that a contingent responsiveness by the mother to her
baby demonstrated reinforcement control of
vocalizations such as babbling, cooing,
coughing, and infant's first two-syllable
sounds.

Although all these finding are short-
term outcomes, they show the important
role of social environment in an infant's
orientation to his world, which is a significant characteristic of cognitive ability. Especially true is the infant's continuous experience with the pleasurable
moments during mother-infant interaction
which form an important climate for cognitive development. A few studies have
measured mother-infant interaction in conjunction with some types of short-term
outcome variables.

Rubenstein (1967) focused on exploratory behavior in five-month-old infants,
and attentiveness in the mother in a study
of forty-four white infants, primarily
from lower-class homes. He found that
"high attentive" mothers were attentive to
their infants in at least 50 percent of
the timed intervals, while "low attentive"
mothers were attentive to the infants less
than 30 percent of the time. "Medium attentive" mothers fell in between. The infants' exploratory behaviors were observed
in a structured situation when they were
six and one-half months old. Infants of
high-attentive mothers spent more time
looking at and vocalizing to the bell and
more time looking at and manipulating the
novel toys in preference to the familiar
toy, and they evidenced more exploratory
behavior than the infants of low or
medium-attentive mothers.

The infant builds up models or schema
on the basis of his past experience (Lewis
and Goldberg 1969, Kagan 1966). When the
infant sees a novel stimulus, he attends
to it longer because it takes time to process new information into his existing
schema. On the other hand, when he sees
a familiar stimulus, he does not attend
to it much because it conforms to his existing schema. This is called "response
decrement." Lewis and Goldberg defined it
as the decrease in fixation time to the
same stimulus over repeated trials. This
decrement is related to a number of variables, such as age, birth condition and
socioeconomic status.

Lewis and Goldberg (1969) also emphasized "response decrement" as a function
of mother-infant interaction. when the
mother was left alone with her infant in

the laboratory, her interaction with the
infant--looking at, smiling, vocalizing,
holding, and touching--were scored every
ten seconds, and the baby's behavior was
also scored. Immediately following a
single blinking light, the infant's response decrement to the light was measured. The result showed that the babies
showing the greatest response decrement
had mothers who interacted a great amount
with their infants. These mothers were also more responsive to their infants' cries
and vocalizations. Lewis and Goldberg
proposed that the importance of the
mother's stimulation to the infant is not
in terms of absolute quantity of stimulation, "but more important, it develops
within the infant the expectancy that his
behavior can affect his environment" (p.
97).

It is noteworthy that the mother
plays an important role as a reinforcer in
specific stimulus-response bonds, so that
she may increase effectively the occurrence of particular reinforced behavior in
the infant. But more important, it develops within the infant the expectancy that
his behavior can affect his environment.
Given expectancy, the infant is motivated
by his past experience (Lewis and Goldberg
1969).

The most critical test for the effect
of mother-infant interaction on cognitive
development can be found in intervention
studies. Levenstein (1970) experimented
with a home-intervention program in which
fifty-four twenty- to forty-three-month-
old children participated. Seventeen
points of I.Q. gain were found among the
experimental group children, who received
thirty-two "verbal interaction stimulation

materials (VISM)" over a seven-month period. In the two control groups there was no
significant gain in I.Q. in the first control group, who received no intervention,
and the second control group who received
the same number of visits, but with a minimum verbal interaction by the toy demon-
strator. In evaluation of this study,
Levenstein suggested that the crucial factor in the child's I.Q. gain was the
change in the mother's behavior toward the
child. However, this writer believes it
not clear whether the crucial factor was
the change in the mother's behavior toward the child through the intervention
period or the "VISM" and the thirty-minute
weekly interaction with the toy demonstra-
tor.

An intervention pilot study by Gordon
(1967) provides a possible answer. The
program was developed to give disadvantaged infants stimulating experiences to
help them achieve higher levels of intellectual development and at the same time
to increase the mothers' feelings of competence and self-worth. One hundred mother-child pairs (children three months to
three years) participated in the program.
Fifteen paraprofessionals, trained as parent educators, visited the homes of the
experimental group once a week for forty
weeks and taught mothers a series of perceptual, motor, auditory, tactile, and
kinesthetic exercises, which the mother
was to introduce to her infant. The experimental infants were tested at six
months on different developmental tests.
Also twenty-five matched-control infants
were tested at six months. A second control group of twenty-five infants was
tested at one year of age. The results

showed a greater development among the experimental group of children as well as maternal positive attitudes and behaviors toward their children during and after intervention.

Gordon (1971), in a study of a "home learning approach to early stimulation," confirmed findings of earlier intervention studies. In addition, he indicated that the longer the children were in the program the better was their performance, with the major increases occurring between two or three years and one year after birth.

The effectiveness of a mother-training program for infant stimulation is also found in the study by Karnes et al. (1970). Working with the mothers of infants in the first and second year of life, they found a significant increase in I.Q. scores of an experimental group over a matched control.

The concept of cognitive development is also introduced and explored in the situations where the mother plays a more direct role. Results of a study by Irwin (1960) demonstrated that working-class mothers who spent fifteen to twenty minutes per day reading to the child during a year-and-a-half period, from thirteen months to thirty months of age, increased vocalization rates in children between seventeen and thirty months of age.

IMPLICATIONS

The literature the writer has reviewed shows that the formation of cognitive skills can reasonably be conceived as developmental in nature and modifiable by variations in the environment (mother). It also contains many suggestions for the important role of the mother, among which are:

Stimulation which is important for the cognitive development of all the infants from any social background. In early years, the infant is responsive primarily to changes in stimulation. The extent to which the mother provides for frequent encounters with a wide variety of situations influences the infant's learning. Frequent and varied stimulation by the mother should be considered in order to maximize the child's growth.

The mother's attention to her infant and the proper response to him are very important to cognitive development. Unless the mother is sensitive in terms of the needs of infant at a given moment for acquisition of cognitive skills, she will not be able to provide a stimulating environment.

Reinforcement of stimulation is important. As previously reviewed in this chapter, repeated training experiences in home intervention programs were effective. Thus, reinforcement should follow behavior fairly quickly to encourage learning of desirable behaviors when they occur.

The concept of cognitive learning in infants can be demonstrated in a wide variety of experiences for young infants through, not only mother-infant interaction, but also by enriching surroundings. Colorful mobiles hung in clear sight, a variety of manipulable toys with pretty bright colors, printed sheets on cribs, and baby clothes with pleasant light colors are all good stimuli. Moderate audi-

tory stimulation is suggested too. In
this spontaneous environment, the infant
is usually involved in his activity and
learning ensues.

SUMMARY

The literature concerning the relation between mother-infant interactions
and cognitive development in infants indicates that social class differences in
maternal stimulation and reinforcement
patterns as well as in early infant experience do exist. Feedback patterns used
by mothers appear important in shaping the
infant's early motivational and cognitive
functioning. Timing, according to developmental levels in mother-infant interaction, is important.

There is need for further study in
the infant's early language environment,
which seems to be critical in cognitive
development. Also longitudinal studies are
necessary for determining the crucial conditions for producing long-term effects in
infant cognitive development.

EPILOGUE

If a man does not keep pace with his
companions, perhaps it is because
he hears a different drummer, let
him step to the music which he hears,
however measured or far away.

Thoreau (1854)

While the material in this book has
been about mother-infant interaction, this
in no way is meant to imply that the father is not important and without influence in the infant's life.

It has been only recently that the
impact of the father on the child's life
has been studied to any great extent, and
most studies have been retrospective ones
on school-age children and young adults.
One exception is a study by Rebelsky and
Hanks (1972) in which they investigated
vocalizations of ten fathers to their infants in the first three months of life.
The researchers reported that the fathers
spent relatively little time interacting
with their infants (an average of 37.7
seconds a day), and the most any father
spent with his infant was 10 minutes, 26
seconds. This is considerably less time

than spent by the mother. Fathers also differed in their vocalization patterns, depending upon the sex of the child.

The father appears to make his impact on the infant in various ways, among which are (1) his own personality and attitude toward children, (2) his attitude and treatment of the mother, (3) his availability in the home to the family and his infant, and (4) his absence in the home.

The symbiotic relationship of the mother-infant has been highlighted in several chapters in this book. While the infant does not discriminate between the biological mother and a mother-surrogate who has attended to him since birth, it seems logical to assume that the mother, who has carried her child through pregnancy and who wants, cherishes, and nurtures him in infancy, will experience that exquisite oneness with him which cannot be accomplished by any other person.

EMOTIONAL DEVELOPMENT

The ways in which maternal attitudes and practices affect ego development, security, emotions, and psychopathology of the infant have been reviewed. That the "state" of the child, that is, his individual makeup and his physiological, neurological, and psychological state at the moment, can influence mother-infant interaction has also been discussed.

The neurological structures subserving emotion have been described and discussed, with special emphasis on the part memories of past events, which have not reached consciousness but can be stored in the "memory system" of the infant and child.

Anna Freud has written that analysts deal with mental representations of drives and not drive activity as such. She says "Equally, we deal not with the happenings in the external world as such but with their repercussions in the mind, i.e., with the form in which they are registered by the child" (A. Freud 1969, p. 174).

It is this writer's opinion that if the brain were as highly organized at birth and in the prenatal period at the cortical level as at the subcortical and midbrain structures, many of our emotional problems would not exist. The infant would be able to rationalize or intellectualize the events that are happening to him; they would not lie in the dark recesses of the unconscious and give rise to fantasies of threats that do not exist.

However, one could look at it another way and say that if we intellectualized everything and all emotions were rational, perhaps we would lose a certain something which makes us able to feel passionately, creatively, and nonverbally in a manner that early cortical control would not allow.

SOCIAL DEVELOPMENT

Sigmund Freud (1921) has written:

And in the development of mankind as a whole, just as in individuals, love alone acts as the civilizing factor in the sense that it brings a change from egoism to altruism (p. 103).

Bettelheim (1950), in his book *Love Is Not Enough,* stresses that love is more than a mere expression of words and physical cuddling; it must be supplemented, he says, by parental planning and efforts to see that the child's needs are met.

The infant has been described in this book as a social being from birth and as an instigator of many mother-infant interactions. When he smiles, cries, babbles, etc., these actions elicit responses from his mother that set in action a chain of events which is self-perpetuating. All of these behaviors, along with an inborn urge to cathect with another, lead to the development of good object relations or attachment.

Through this reciprocal relationship, the infant learns that certain behaviors produce smiles and other gestures of approval from his mother and others in his environment. Conversely, other behaviors produce scowls and disapproving responses from his mother. To keep her love, he learns gradually to give up his own bodily pleasures for the love of another, and whether it is through imitation, identification, conditioning, or whatever, he becomes eventually less egocentric and more altruistic in his actions and viewpoints.

The mere presence of the mother is not sufficient to evoke these responses, but an attentive and responsive mother can do so. As the infant becomes more mobile, he requires a new set of maternal responses and behaviors. He needs demands and expectations commensurate with his level of development, and through a warm, ac-

cepting atmosphere, along with consistency
of discipline, he eventually develops internal controls. It is small wonder that
Freud (1938) viewed early mother-infant
relationship as the prototype of all future relationships.

PERCEPTUAL-COGNITIVE DEVELOPMENT

All of the infant's senses are functioning at birth, and through his senses
he learns about the world around him.
Some senses are more highly developed than
others; and some, such as form perception,
take years to develop.

The importance of the role of the
mother in aiding in sensory discrimination is well documented. In fact Fantz
(1966) has said he could distinguish between home-reared and institution-reared
infants by their visual responses in the
second year of life. Korner and Grobstein
(1966) and Korner (1971) have found that
when a crying baby is picked up and held
at the shoulder his crying stops and he
becomes visually alert, scanning the environment. Other such examples have been
given in the text.

Germane to effective cognitive development are stimulation which is appropriate to the child's individual makeup
and his level of development, and maternal factors of warmth, acceptance, and
autonomy. Again, autonomy must be geared
to the age level of the child and his capabilities, along with encouragement,
gratifiying communication, and positive
reinforcement (Hamilton, 1972). Hamilton
says: "Thus a variant of 'perceptual dep-

rivation,' as well as experiences of insecurity and anxiety may affect the
child's cognitive development" (1972,
p. 147).

Maternal factors have also been found
to influence cognitive style, that is,
field dependence and field-independence.
Witkin (1971) found infants who were less
differentiated (field dependent) had mothers who were indifferent and insensitive
to their infants' distress or who acted
hastily out of their own anxiety, which
spilled over onto the infant. They also
tended to respond to the baby in a global
manner, handling his body with insensitiv-
ity and in a way that was more satisfying
to them than to the infant.

Yarrow (1963) found that the amount
and especially the appropriateness of the
stimulation given to the infant was highly
correlated with I.Q. He also found experiences and toys given to the infant which
were adapted to his age level and abilities correlated highly with I.Q. (.69).
Clarke-Stewart (1973) found the complexity
of the child's cognitive development was
related to maternal time spent with the
infant in playing with objects but was not
related to the mere presence with objects
in the environment. She also found "social
and visual" attention by the mother to increase a child's intellectual competence.

In conclusion, it appears that the
emotional, social, and perceptual-
cognitive areas of development are all in-
tertwined, and it is impossible to separate one from the other in the total development of the child. The importance of
the mother as a mediator of the environment and the pervasive effects of mother-
infant interaction are the most important

determinants of the unfolding of the individual's potential development. Through the effectiveness of these interactions, he can develop to his fullest potential.

REFERENCES

Aichhorn, A. 1925. *Wayward youth*. New York: Viking Press.

Ainsworth, M. D. 1962. The effects of maternal deprivation: A review of findings and controversy in the context of research strategy. In *Deprivation of maternal care: A reassessment of its effects*, Public Health Papers No. 14. Geneva: World Health Organization, pp. 97-165.

------. 1963. The development of infant-mother interaction among the Ganda. In *Determinants of infant behavior*, vol. 2, edited by B. M. Foss. New York: Wiley.

------. 1964. Patterns of attachment behavior shown by the infant in interaction with his mothers. *Merrill-Palmer Quarterly* 10: 51-58.

------. 1967. *Infancy in Uganda: Care and growth of love*. Baltimore: Johns Hopkins University Press.

------. 1969. Object relations, dependency, and attachment: A theoretical review of infant-mother relationship. *Child Development* 40: 469-1027.

------. 1973. The development of mother-infant attachment. In *Review of child development research,* edited by B. A. Caldwell and H. N. Ricciuti. Chicago: University of Chicago Press.

Aldrich, C. A. 1946. A developmental graph for the first year of life. *Journal of Pediatrics* 29: 304.

Ambrose, J. A. 1963. The concept of a critical period for the development of social responsiveness in early human infancy. In *Determinants of infant behavior,* vol. 2, edited by B. M. Foss. New York: Wiley.

Baldwin, A. L. 1967. *Theories of child development.* New York: Wiley.

Ban, P. L., and Lewis, M. 1974. Mothers and fathers, girls and boys: Attachment behavior in the one-year-old. *Merrill-Palmer Quarterly* 20: 195-204.

Baron, R. M. 1970. The SRS model as a predictor of Negro responsiveness to reinforcement. *Journal of Social Issues* 16: 61-81.

Bartley, S. H. 1969. *Principles of perception.* New York: Harper and Row.

Baumrind, D. 1972. Some thoughts about children. In *Influence of human development,* edited by U. Bronfenbrenner.

Hinsdale, Ill.: Dryden Press.

Bayley, N. 1965. Comparisons of mental and motor test scores for ages 1-15 months by sex, birth order, race, geographical location, and education of parents. *Child Development* 36: 379-411.

Bayley, N., and Schaefer, E. S. 1964. Correlations of maternal and child behaviors with the development of mental abilities: Data from the Berkely growth study. *Monographs of the Society for Research in Child Development 29* (Serial No. 97).

Beckwith, L. 1972. Relationships between infants' social behavior and their mothers' behavior. *Child development* 43: 397-411.

Beiser, B. M. 1965. Poverty, social disintegration and personality. *Journal of Social Issues* 21: 56-78.

Bell, R. Q. 1971. Stimulus control of parent or caretaker behavior of offspring. *Developmental Psychology* 4: 63-71.

Bell, R. Q., Weller, G. M., and Waldrop, M. F. 1971. Newborn and preschooler: Organization of behavior and relations between periods. *Monographs of the Society for Research in Child Development 36* (Serial No. 142).

Bell, S. M. 1970. The development of the concept of object as related to infant-mother attachment. *Child Development* 41: 291-310.

Bellak, L. 1963. Acting out: Conceptual and therapeutic considerations. *American Journal of Psychotherapy* 17: 375-389.

Benedek, T. 1949. The psychosomatic implications of the primary unit: Mother-child. *American Journal of Orthopsychiatry* 19: 642-654.

------. 1956. Toward the biology of the depressive constellation. *Journal of the American Psychoanalytic Association* 4: 389-397.

Benjamin, J. D. 1963. Further comments on some developmental aspects of anxiety. In *Counterpoint: Libidinal object and subject,* edited by H. S. Gaskil. New York: International Universities Press.

------. 1965. Developmental biology and psychoanalysis. In *Psychoanalysis and current biological thought,* edited by N. S. Greenfield and W. C. Lewis. Madison: University of Wisconsin Press.

Bergman, P., and Escalona, S. K. 1949. Unusual sensitivities in very young children. *The Psychoanalytic Study of the Child* 3-4: 33-352.

Berlyne, D. E. 1960. *Conflict, arousal, and curiosity.* New York: McGraw-Hill.

Bettelheim, B. 1950. *Love is not enough.* New York: Free Press.

------. 1969. *The children of the dream.* London: Macmillan.

Bijou, S. W., and Baer, D. M. 1961. *Child development: A systematic and empirical theory*, vol. 1. New York: Appleton-Century-Crofts.

------. 1965. *Child Development: The universal stage of infancy*, vol. 2. New York: Appleton-Century-Crofts.

Bindra, D. 1974. A motivational view of learning, performance, and behavior modification. *Psychological Review* 81: 199-213.

Blackham, G. J., and Silberman, A. 1971. *Modification of child behavior*. Belmont, Calif.: Wadsworth.

Blehar, M. P. 1973. Attachment and day care. Reported in Ainsworth, M. D. The development of infant-mother attachment. In *Review of child development research*, vol. 3, edited by B. A. Caldwell and H. R. Ricciuti. Chicago: University of Chicago Press.

Bloom, B. S. 1965. *Stability and change in human characteristics*. New York: Wiley.

Bower, T. G. R. 1964. Discrimination of depth in premotor infants. *Psychonomic Science* 1: 368.

------. 1965. Stimulus variables determining space perception in infants. *Science* 149: 88-89.

------. 1971. The object in the world of the infant. *Scientific American* 225: 30-38.

Bowlby, J. 1944. Forty-four juvenile children: Their character and home life.
International Journal of Psychoanalysis
25: 19-52; 107-127.

------. 1951. *Maternal care and mental
health*. Geneva: World Health Organization.

------. 1958. The nature of the child's
tie to his mother. *International Journal of Psychoanalysis* 39: 350-373.

------. 1960. Grief and mourning in infancy and early childhood. In *The Psychoanalytic Study of the Child*. New York:
International Universitites Press, 9-
52.

------. 1969. *Attachment and loss*, vol. 1.
New York: Basic Books.

Brackbill, Y. 1958. Extinction of the smiling response in infants as a function
of reinforcement schedule. *Child Development* 29: 115-124.

Brazelton, T. B. 1969. *Infants and mothers*. New York: Delacorte.

Brackenridge, M. E., and Murphy, M. N.
1969. *Growth and development of the
young child*. Philadelphia: W. B. Saun-
ders.

Brody, S. 1956. *Patterns of mothering*. New
York: International Universities Press.

Brody, S. and Axelrad, S. A. 1970. *Anxiety
and ego formation in infancy*. New York:
International Universities Press.

Bronfenbrenner, U. 1972. *Influences of human development*. Hinsdale, Ill.: Dryden.

Bruner, J. S. 1964. The course of cognitive growth. *American Psychologist* 19: 1-15.

------. 1970. Discussion: Infant education as viewed by a psychologist. In *Education of the infant and young child*, edited by V. H. Denenberg. New York: Academic Press.

------. 1971 Overview of development and day care. In *Day care: Resource for direction*, edited by E. H. Grotberg. U. S. Government Printing Office, Washington, D. C., pp. 90-108.

Buhler, C. 1930. *The first year of life*. Translated by Pearl Greenberg and Rowena Ripin. New York: John Day.

Cairns, R. B. 1972. Attachment and dependency: A psychobiological and social-learning synthesis. In *Attachment and dependency*, edited by J. L. Gewirtz. Washington, D. C.: V. H. Winston.

Caldwell, B. M. 1962. The usefulness of the critical period hypothesis in the study of filiative behavior. *Merrill-Palmer Quarterly* 8: 229-242.

------. 1964a. The effects of infant care. In *Review of child development research*, vol. 1, edited by M. L. Hoffman and L. W. Hoffman. New York: Russell Sage Foundation, pp. 9-87.

------. 1964*b*. Mother-infant interaction during the first year of life. *Merrill-Palmer Quarterly* 10: 119-128.

------. 1972. What does research teach us about day care for children under three? *Children Today* 1: 6-11.

Caldwell, B. M., and Richmond, J. B. 1968. The children's center in Syracuse, New York. In *Early child care*, edited by L. L. Dittmann. New York: Atherton Press.

Caldwell, B. M., Wright, C. M., Honig, A., and Tannenbaum, J. 1970. Infant day care and attachment. *American Journal of Orthopsychiatry* 40: 397-412.

Call, J. D. 1964. Newborn approach behavior and early ego development. *International Journal of Psychoanalysis* 45: 286-294.

------. 1968. Lap and finger play in infancy, implications for ego development. *International Journal of Psychoanalysis* 49: 375-378.

Casler, L. 1968. Perceptual deprivation in institutional settings. In *Early experience and behavior*, edited by G. Newton and S. Levine. Springfield: Charles Thomas.

Cattell, R. B., and Scheier, I. H. 1963. *Handbook for the IPAT anxiety scale questionnaire*. Champaign, Ill.: Institute of Personality and Ability Testing.

Child Welfare League of America. 1969. *Standards for day care service.* New York: Child Welfare League of America.

Clarke-Stewart, K. A. 1973. Interactions between mothers and their young children: Characteristics and consequences. *Monographs of the Society for Research in Child Development 38* (Serial No. 153).

Cohen, L. J., and Campos, J. J. 1974. Father, mother, and stranger as elicitors of attachment behaviors in infancy. *Developmental Psychology 10:* 146-154.

Dekaban, A. 1959. *Neurology in infancy.* Baltimore: Williams and Wilkins.

Denenberg, V. H. 1964. Critical periods, stimulus input, and emotional reactivity: A theory of infantile stimulation. *Psychological Review 71:* 335-351.

------. 1967. Stimulation in infancy, emotional reactivity, and exploratory behavior. In *Biology and behavior: Neurophysiology and emotion,* edited by D. C. Glass. New York: Russell Sage Foundation.

------. 1969. Animal studies of early experience: Some principles which have implications for human development. In *Minnesota symposia on child psychology,* edited by J. P. Hill. Minneapolis: University of Minnesota Press.

Dennis, W. 1960. Causes of retardation among institutional children: Iran. *Journal of Genetic Psychology 96:* 47-59.

Dennis, W. and Najarian, P. 1957. Infant development under environmental handicap. *Psychological Monographs* 71: 1-13.

Des Lauriers, A. M. 1967. The schizophrenic child. *Archives of General Psychiatry* 16: 194-201.

Deutsch, C. P. 1964. Auditory discrimination and learning: Social factors. *Merrill-Palmer Quarterly* 10: 277-296.

Dreger, R. M., and Miller, K. S. 1968. Comparative psychological studies of Negroes and whites in the United States: 1959-1965. *Psychological Bulletin Monograph Supplement* 70: no. 3, part 2.

Eisenberg, R. B. 1969. Auditory behavior in the human neonate: Functional properties of sound and their ontogenetic implications. *International Audiology* 8: 34-45.

Emerson, R. W. 1903. *Essays*. Cambridge: Riverside Press.

Engen, T., Lipsitt, L. P., and Kaye, H. 1963. Olfactory response and adaptation in the human neonate. *Journal of Comparative Physiological Psychology* 56: 73-77.

Erikson, E. H. 1950. Growth and crises of the healthy personality. In *Symposium on the healthy personality*, edited by M. J. E. Senn. New York: Josiah Macy, Jr., Foundation, pp. 91-120.

------. 1959. Identity and the life cycle.

Psychological Issues, Monograph 1, no. 1: 1-171.

------. 1963. *Childhood and society.* 2d ed. New York: W. W. Norton.

Escalona, S. K. 1952. Emotional development in the first year of life. In *Problems of infancy and childhood,* edited by M. J. E. Senn. New York: Josiah Macy, Jr., Foundation, pp. 97-137.

------. 1963. patterns of infantile experience and the developmental process. *The Psychoanalytic Study of the Child* 18: 197-244.

------. 1965. Some determinants of individual differences. *Transactions of the New York Academy. Science* 27: 802-816.

------. 1967. Developmental needs of children under two-and-a-half years old. In *On Rearing Infants and Young Children in Institutions,* edited by H. L. Witmer. Washington, D. C.: United States Department of Health, Education and Welfare, Children's Bureau, Research Reports: 7-13.

------. 1968. *The roots of individuality: Normal patterns of development in infancy.* Chicago: Aldine.

------. 1973. Basic modes of social interaction: Their emergence and patterning during the first two years of life. *Merrill-Palmer Quarterly* 19: 205-232.

Estes, W. K. 1972. Reinforcement in human

behavior. *American Scientist* 60: 723-729.

Etzel, B. C., and Gewirtz, J. L. 1967. Experimental modification of caretaker-maintained high-rate operant crying in a 6- and 20-week old infant (Infants Tyrannotearus): Extinction of crying with reinforcement of eye contact and smiling. *Journal of Experimental Child Psychology* 5: 303-317.

Fantz, R. L. 1961. The origin of form perception. *Scientific American* 204: 66-72.

------. 1963. Pattern vision in newborn infants. *Science* 140: 296-297.

------. 1965. Pattern discrimination and selective attention as determinants of perceptual development from birth. In *Perceptual development in children,* edited by A. H. Kidd and J. L. Rivoire. New York: International Universities Press.

------. 1966. The crucial early influence: Mother love or environmental stimulation? *American Journal of Orthopsychiatry* 36: 330-331.

Fantz, R. L., and Nevis, S. 1967. Pattern preferences and perceptual cognitive development in early infancy. *Merrill-Palmer Quarterly* 13: 77-108.

Fenichel, O. 1945. *The psychoanalytic theory of neurosis.* New York: W. W. Norton.

Ferguson, L. 1971. Origins of social development in fancy. *Merrill-Palmer Quarterly* 17: 119-137.

Fish, B., Shapiro, T., Halpern, F., and Wile, R. 1965. The prediction of schizophrenia in infancy. *American Journal of Psychiatry* 121: 768-775.

Fiske, D. W., and Maddi, S. R. 1961. *Functions of varied experience*. Homewood, Ill.: Dorsey Press.

Flint, B. M. 1959. *The security of infants*. Toronto: University of Toronto Press.

Fowler, W. 1962. Cognitive learning in infancy and early childhood. *Psychological Bulletin* 59: 116-152.

------. 1964. Structure dimensions of the learning process in early reading. *Child Development* 35: 1093-1104.

------. 1968. The effect of early stimulation on the emergence of cognitive processes. In *Early education: Report of research and action,* edited by R. D. Hess and R. M. Bear. Chicago: Aldine.

------. 1969. The effect of early stimulation: the problem of focus in developmental stimulation. *Merrill-Palmer Quarterly* 15: 157-170.

------. 1972. A developmental learning approach to infant care in a group setting. *Merrill-Palmer Quarterly* 18: 146-175.

Fraiberg, S. and Freedman, D. A. 1964. Studies in the ego development of the congenitally blind. *The Psychoanalytic Study of the Child* 19: 113-169.

Frank, L. 1966. *On the importance of infancy.* New York: Random House.

Freedman, D. A. 1972. On the limits of the effectiveness of psychoanalysis: Early ego and somatic disturbances. *International Journal of Psychoanalysis* 53: 363-370.

Freud, A. 1946. The psychoanalytic study of infantile feeding disturbances. *The Psychoanalytic Study of the Child* 2: 119-132.

------. 1963. The concept of developmental lines. *The Psychoanalytic Study of the Child* 18: 245-256.

------. 1966 (1936). *The writings of Anna Freud: The ego and mechanisms of defense,* vol. 2. New York: International Universities Press.

------. 1968. Indications and contraindications for child analysis. *The Psychoanalytic Study of the Child* 23: 37-40.

------. 1969. *The writings of Anna Freud,* vol. 5. New York: International Universities Press.

Freud, S. 1925. On narcissism: An introduction. In *Collected papers,* vol. 4, edited by E. Sanes. London: Hogarth Press, pp. 30-59.

------. 1938 (1905). Three contributions to the theory of sex. In *Basic writings of Sigmund Freud*. New York: Random House: 553-629.

------. 1949. *An outline of psychoanalysis*. New York: W. W. Norton.

------. 1955 (1921). *Group psychology and the analysis of the ego*. London: Hogarth Press.

------. 1957 (1905). *Three essays on sexuality*. London: Hogarth Press.

------. 1959 (1926). *Inhibitions, symptoms and anxiety*. London: Hogarth Press.

Friedlander, B. Z. 1970. Receptive language development in infancy: Issues and problems. *Merrill-Palmer Quarterly* 16: 7-51.

Fries, M. E. 1935. Interrelationship of physical, mental and emotional life of a child from birth to four years of age. *American Journal of Diseases of Children* 49: 1546-1563.

Garner, A. M., and Wenar, C. G. 1959. *The mother-child interaction in psychosomatic disorders*. Urbana, Ill.: University of Illinois Press.

Gediman, H. K. 1971. The concept of stimulus barrier: Its review and reformulation as an adaptive ego function. *International Journal of Psychoanalysis* 52: 243-257.

Gesell, A. 1950. Infant vision. *Scientific American* 182.

Gesell, A., and Armatruda, C. S. 1945. *The embryology of behavior.* New York: Harper and Brothers.

------. 1947. *Developmental diagnosis: Normal and abnormal child development.* 2nd ed. New York: Hoeber.

Gewirtz, J. L. 1968. On designing the functional environment of the child to facilitate behavioral development. In *Early child care,* edited by L. L. Dittmann. New York: Atherton Press: 169-213.

Gibson, E. J. 1969. *Principles of perceptual learning and development.* New York: Appleton-Century-Crofts.

Gibson, E. J., and Walk, R. D. 1960. The visual cliff. *Scientific American* 202: 64-71.

Ginandes, S. C. 1964. Children who are sent away. *American Academy of Child Psychiatry* 3: 68-88.

Goldberg, S. 1972. Infant care and growth in urban Zambia. *Human Development* 15: 77-89.

Goldberg, S., and Lewis, M. 1969. Play behavior in the year-old infant: Early sex differences. *Child Development* 40: 21-31.

Golden, M., and Birns, B. 1968. Social class and cognitive development in in-

fancy. *Merrill-Palmer Quarterly* 14:
139-149.

Goldfarb, W. 1943a. The effects of early
institutional care on adolescent personality. *Journal of Experimental Education* 12: 106.

------. 1943b. Infant rearing and problem
behavior. *American Journal of Orthopsychiatry* 13: 249-265.

------. 1945. Effects of psychological
deprivation in infancy and subsequent
stimulation. *American Journal of Psychiatry* 102: 18-33.

------. 1955. Emotional and intellectual
consequences of psychological depriva-
tion in infancy. A revaluation. In
Psychopathology of childhood, edited by
P. H. Hoch and J. Zubin. Grune and
Stratton: 105-119.

------. 1961. *Childhood schizophrenia.*
Cambridge, Mass.: Harvard University
Press.

Goldman-Eisler, F. 1953. Breastfeeding and
character formation. In *Personality in
nature, society, and culture,* edited by
C. Kluckhohn and H. Murray. New York:
Knopf: 146-184.

Gordon, I. J. 1967. *A parent education approach to provision for the culturally
disadvantaged: Final report.* Gainesville, Fla.: Institute for Development
of Human Resources, University of Florida.

------. 1971. *A home learning center approach to early stimulation.* Gainesville, Fla.: Institute for Development of Human Resources, University of Florida.

Gouin Décarie, T. D., Goulet, J., Brossard, M. D., Rafman, S., and Shaffran, R. 1974. *The infant's reaction to strangers.* New York: International Universities Press.

Graham, F. K., Ernhart, C. B., Craft, M., and Berman, P. W. 1963. Brain injury in the preschool child: Some development considerations: 1. Performance of normal children. *Psychological Monographs* 77: 1-16.

Greenacre, P. 1941. The predisposition to anxiety. *The Psychoanalytic Quarterly* 10: 66-94.

------. 1960. Considerations regarding the parent-infant relationship. *The International Journal of Psychoanalysis* 41: 571-581.

Greenberg, D., Urgiris, I., and Hunt, J. McV. 1968. Hastening the development of the blink-response with looking. *Journal of Genetic Psychology* 113: 167-176.

Greenberg, N. H. 1965. Developmental effects of stimulation during early infancy: Some conceptual and methodological considerations. *Annals of the New York Academy of Sciences* 118: 831-859.

------. Atypical behavior during infancy: Infant development in relation to the behavior and personality of the mother. In *The child in his family,* edited by E. J. Anthony and C. Koupernik. New York: Wiley.

Greene, W. A. 1958. Early object relations, somatic, affective, and personal. *Journal of Nervous and Mental Disease* 126: 225-253.

Greenman, G. W. 1963. Visual behavior of newborn infants. In *Modern perspective in child development,* edited by A. Solnit and S. Provence. New York: International Universities Press.

Griffiths, R. 1954. *The abilities of babies.* New York: McGraw-Hill.

Grotberg, E. H. 1971. *Day care: Resources for decisions.* Washington, D. C.: U. S. Government Printing Office.

Hamilton, V. 1972. Maternal rejection and conservation: An analysis of sub-optimal cognitions. *Journal of Child Psychology* 13: 147-166.

Harlow, H. F. 1958. The nature of love. *American Psychologist* 13: 673-685.

------. 1963. The maternal affectional system. In *Determinants of infant behavior, vol 2,* edited by B. M. Foss. New York: Wiley.

Harlow, H. F., and Harlow, M. K. 1962. Social deprivation in monkeys. *Scientific American* 207: 136-144.

------. 1966. Learning to love. *American*

Scientist 54: 244-272.

Harris, T. A. 1969. *I'm O.K., You're O.K. A practical guide to transactional analysis*. New York: Harper and Row.

Hartman, H. 1958. *Ego psychology and the problem of adaptation*. New York: International Universities Press.

Hebb, D. O. 1949. *The organization of behavior*. New York: Wiley.

------. 1955. Drives and the conceptual nervous system. *Psychological Review* 62: 243-254.

Heinicke, C. M., Friedman, D., Prescott, E., Puncel, C., and Sale, J. S. 1973. The organization of day care: Considerations relating to the mental health of child and family. *American Journal of Orthopsychiatry* 43: 8-22.

Heinstein, M. I. 1963. Behavioral correlates of breast-bottle regimes under varying parent-infant relationships. *Monographs of the Society for Research in Child Development* 28 (Serial No. 88).

Hershenson, M. 1964. Visual discrimination in the human newborn. *Journal of Comparative Physiological Psychology* 58: 270-276.

------. 1967. Development of the perception of form. *Psychological Bulletin* 67: 326-336.

Hershenson, M., Munsinger, H., and Kessen, W. 1965. Preference for shapes of intermediate variability in the newborn human. *Science* 147: 630-631.

Hess, R., and Shipman, V. 1965. Early experience in the socialization of cognitive modes in children. *Child Development* 36: 869-886.

------. 1967. Cognitive elements in maternal behavior. In *Minnesota symposia on child psychology,* edited by J. P. Hill. Minneapolis: University of Minnesota Press: 396-409.

Hill, D. 1964. Aggression and mental illness. In *Natural history of aggression,* edited by J. D. Carthy and F. J. Ebling. New York: Academic Press: 91-99.

Hollingshead, A. B., and Redlich, F. C. 1958. *Social class and mental illness.* New York: Wiley.

Holt, R. R. 1965. A review of some of Freud's biological assumptions and their influence on his theories. In *Psychoanalysis and current biological thought,* edited by N. S. Greenfield and W. C. Lewis. Madison: University of Wisconsin Press.

Honzik, M. P. 1964. Personality consistency and change: Some comments on papers by Bayley, MacFarlane, Moss and Kagan, and Murphy. *Vita Humana* 7: 139-142.

Horowitz, F. P. 1967. Social reinforcements on child behavior. In *The young child,* edited by W. W. Hartup and N. L. Smothergill. Washington, D. C.: National Association for the Education of Young Children.

------. 1968. Infant learning and development: Retrospect and prospect. *Merrill-
Palmer Quarterly* 14: 101-120.

Horowitz, F. P., and Paden, L. Y. 1973.
The effectiveness of environmental interaction programs. In *Review of child
development and research,* edited by
B. A. Caldwell and H. N. Ricciuti. Chicago: University of Chicago Press.

Hubel, D. H., and Wiesel, T. N. 1963. Receptive fields of cells in the striate
cortex of very young, visually inex-
perienced kittens. *Journal of Neurophysiology* 26: 996-1002.

Hunt, J. McV. 1961. *Intelligence and experience.* New York: Ronald Press.

------. 1964. The psychological basis for
using preschool enrichment as an anti-
dote for cultural deprivation. *Merrill-
Palmer Quarterly* 10: 209-248.

------. 1971. Parent and child centers:
Their basis in the behavioral and edu-
cational sciences. *American Journal of
Orthopsychiatry* 41: 13-38.

Hutt, C. 1970. Specific and diversive exploration. In *Advances in child development and behavior,* vol. 5, edited by
H. W. Reece and L. P. Lipsitt. New
York: Academic Press: 120-172.

Irwin, O. C. 1960. Infant speech. Effect
of systematic reading of stories. *Journal of Speech and Hearing Research* 3:
187-190.

Jacobson, Edith. 1964. *The self and the object world*. New York: International Universities Press.

James, Martin. 1962. Infantile narcistic trauma. Observations on Winnicott's work in infant care and child development. *International Journal of Psychoanalysis* 33: 69-77.

Jeffrey, W. E. 1965. The orienting reflex and attention in cognitive development. *Psychological Review* 75: 323-334.

Jourard, S. M. 1968. *Disclosing man to himself*. Princeton: Van Nostrand.

Kagan, J. 1965. Reflection-impulsivity and reading ability in primary grade children. *Child Development* 36: 609-628.

------. 1966. A developmental approach to conceptual growth. In *Analyses of concept learning,* edited by H. J. Klausmeier and C. W. Harris. New York: Academic Press.

------. 1969. Continuity in cognitive development during the first year. *Merrill-Palmer Quarterly* 15: 101-119.

------. 1971. *Change and continuity in infancy*. New York: Wiley.

------. 1972. Do infants think? *Scientific American* 226: 74-81.

Kagan, J., Henker, B. A., Hen-Tov, A., Levine, J., and Lewis, M. 1966. Infants' differential reactions to familiar and distorted faces. *Child Development* 37:

519-532.

Kagan, J. and Lewis, M. 1965. Studies of attention in the human infant. *Merrill-Palmer Quarterly* 11: 95-127.

Karnes, M. B., Teska, J. A., Hodgins, S., and Badger, E. D. 1970. Educational intervention at home by mothers of disadvantaged infants. *Child Development,* 41: 925-935.

Kessen, W. 1967. Sucking and looking: Two organized congenital patterns of behavior in the human newborn. In *Early behavior: Comparative and developmental approaches,* edited by H. W. Stevenson, E. H. Hess, and H. L. Rheingold.

Kessen, W., Haith, M. M., and Salapatek, P. H. 1970. Human infancy. In *Carmichael's manual of child psychology,* edited by P. H. Mussen.

Klaus, R. A., and Gray, S. W. 1968. The early training project for disadvantaged children: A report after five years. *Monographs of the Society for Research in Child Development 33* (Serial No. 120).

Kleeman, J. A. 1967. The peek-a-boo game: Part I. Its origins, meanings and related phenomena in the first year. *Psychoanalytic Study of the Child* 22: 239-273.

Klein, J. W. 1972. Educational component of day care. *Children Today* 1: 3-5.

Klein, M. 1964. *Contributions to psycho-*

analysis: 1912-1945. New York: McGraw-Hill.

Kohen-Raz, R. 1968. Mental and motor development of kibbutz, institutionalized, and home-reared infants in Israel. *Child Development* 39: 489-504.

Korner, A. 1971. Individual differences at birth: Implications for early experience and later development. *American Journal of Orthopsychiatry* 41: 608-619.

Korner, A., and Grobstein, R. 1966. Visual alertness as related to soothing in neonates: Implications for maternal stimulation and early deprivation. *Child Development* 37: 867-876.

Landauer, T. K., and Whiting, J. W. 1964. Infantile stimulation and adult stature of human males. *American Anthropologist* 66: 1007-1028.

Lashley, K. S. 1954. Dynamic process in perception. In *Brain mechanisms and consciousness; a symposium,* edited by E. D. Adrian, F. Brenner, and H. H. Jasper. Oxford: Blackwell:

Lazar, I., and Rosenberg, M. E. Day care in America. In *Day care: Resource for decision,* edited by E. H. Grothberg. Washington, D. C.: U. S. Government Printing Office: 59-87.

Leuba, C. 1955. Toward some integration of learning theories: The concept of optimal stimulation. *Psychological Reports* 1: 27-33.

Levenstein, P. 1970. Cognitive growth in preschoolers through verbal interaction with mothers. *American Journal of Orthopsychiatry* 40: 426-432.

Levine, S., Haltmeyer, G. C., Karas, G. G., and Denenberg, V. H. 1967. Physiological and behavioral effects of infantile stimulation. *Physiology and Behavior* 2: 55-59.

Levy, D. M. 1928. Finger-sucking and accessory movements in early infancy: An etiologic study. *American Journal of Psychiatry* 7: 881-918.

------. 1951. The deprived and the indulged forms of psychopathic personality. *American Journal of Orthopsychiatry* 21: 250-254.

Lewis, M. 1967. Infant attention: Response decrement as a measure of cognitive processes, or what's new, Baby Jane? Paper presented at the Society for Research in Child Development Symposium on the role of attention in cognitive development, New York.

------. 1972. State as an infant-environment interaction: An analysis of mother-infant interaction as a function of sex. *Merrill-Palmer Quarterly* 18: 95-121.

Lewis, M., and Goldberg, S. 1969. Perceptual-cognitive development in infancy: A generalized expectancy model as a function of the mother-infant interaction. *Merrill-Palmer Quarterly* 15: 81-100.

Lewis, M., and Wilson, C. D. 1972. Infant development in lower-class American families. *Human Development* 15: 112-127.

Liley, M. 1965. Discovering old miracles. *McCall's* August: 92-93; 134-136.

Lipsitt, L. P. 1963. Learning in the first year of life. In *Advances in child development and behavior*, edited by L. P. Lipsitt and C. C. Spikes. New York: Academic Press.

------. 1966. Learning process of newborns. *Merrill-Palmer Quarterly* 12: 45-72.

McCall, R. B., and Kagan, J. 1967. Attention in the infant: Effects of complexity, contour, perimeter, and familiarity. *Child Development* 38: 939-952.

Maccoby, E. E. 1958. Children and working mothers. *Children* 5: 83-89.

McGrade, B. J., Kessen, W., and Leutzendorff, A. 1965. Activity in the human newborn as related to delivery difficulty. *Child Development* 36: 73-79.

MacLean, P. D. 1940. Psychosomatic disease and the "visceral brain": Recent developments bearing on the Papez theory of emotion. *Psychosomatic Medicine* 11: 338-353.

Madsen, C. H., Jr., and Madsen, C. K. 1970. *Teaching and discipline: Behavioral principles toward a positive approach.* Boston: Allyn and Bacon, Inc.

Magoun, H. W. 1963. *The waking brain.* Springfield, Ill.: Charles C. Thomas.

Mahler, M. S. 1952. On child psychosis and schizophrenia. Autistic and symbiotic infantile psychosis. *Psychoanalytic Study of the Child* 7: 286-305.

------. 1960. Symposium on psychotic object relationships III. Perceptual de-differentiation and psychotic relationship. *International Journal of Psychoanalysis* 41: 548-553.

------. 1963. Thoughts about development and individuation. *Psychoanalytic Study of the Child* 18: 307-324.

------. 1968. *On human symbiosis and the vicissitudes of individuation,* vol. 1. *Infantile psychosis.* New York: International Universities Press.

Mead, M. 1962. A cultural anthropologist's approach to maternal deprivation. In *Deprivation of maternal care,* public health paper no. 14. Geneva: World Health Organization: 45-62.

Melzack, R. 1961. The perception of pain. *Scientific American* 204: 1-9.

Messinger, J. 1965. Discussion. In *Children in collectives,* edited by P. Neubauer. Springfield, Ill.: Charles C. Thomas.

Montagu, A. 1950. Constitutional and prenatal factors in infant and child care. In *Symposium on the healthy personality,* edited by M. J. Senn. New York:

Josiah Macy, Jr., Foundation.

------. 1965. *Life before birth*. New York: New American Library.

------. 1971. *Touching*. New York: Harper and Row.

Moore, T. 1964. Children of full-time and part-time mothers. *International Journal of Social Psychiatry* 2: 1-10.

------. 1969. Stress in normal childhood. *Human Relations* 22: 235-250.

Morgan, G. A., and Ricciuti, H. N. 1969. Infants' responses to strangers during the first year. In *Determinants of infant behavior,* vol. 4, edited by B. M. Foss. London: Methuen: 253-272.

Morton, J. R. C., Denenberg, V. H., and Zarrow, M. X. 1963. Modification of sexual development through stimulation in infancy. *Endocrinology* 72: 439-442.

Moruzzi, G., and Magoun, H. W. 1949. Brain stem reticular formation and activation of the EEG. *Electroencephalography and Neurophysiology* 1: 455-473.

Moss, H. A. 1967. Sex, age, and state as determinants of mother-infant interaction. *Merrill-Palmer Quarterly,* 13: 19-36.

Moss, H. A., and Robson, K. S. 1968. Maternal influences in early visual behavior. *Child Development* 39: 401-408.

Murphy, L. B. 1962. *The widening world of childhood*. New York: Basic Books.

------. 1968. Individualization of child care and its relation to environment. In *Early child care: the new perspectives,* edited by L. L. Dittmann. New York: Atherton Press.

------. 1973. Development in the first year of life: Ego and drive development in relation to the mother-infant tie. In *The competent infant, research and comentary,* edited by L. L. Stone, H. T. Smith, and L. B. Murphy. New York: Basic Books.

Newton, N. 1963. Emotions of pregnancy. *Clinical Obstetrics and Gynecology* 66: 39-668.

Ornitz, E. M. 1969. Disorders of perception common to early infantile autism and schizophrenia. *Psychiatry* 10: 259-274.

Ornitz, E., and Ritvo, E. R. 1968. Perceptual inconsistency in early infantile autism. *Archives of General Psychiatry* 18: 76-98.

Orthner, B. F. 1969. Parental religiosity and attitudes concerning children. Unpublished master's thesis. Florida State University.

Osotsky, J. D., and Danzer, B. 1974. Relationship between neonatal characteristics and mother infant interaction. *Developmental Psychology* 10: 124-130.

Ottinger, R., and Simmons, J. E. 1964. Behavior of human neonates and prenatal maternal anxiety. *Psychological Report,*

14: 391-394.

Papez, J. W. 1937. A proposed mechanism of emotion. *Archives of Neurology and Psychiatry* 38: 725-749.

Pavlov, I. P. 1927 (1910). *Conditioned Reflexes*. London: Oxford University Press.

Pearson, L., and Welch, L. 1966. Conceptual impulsivity and inductive reasoning. *Child Development* 37: 583-594.

Peller, L. 1954. Libidinal development and play. *Psychoanalytic Study of the Child* 9: 178-197.

Phillips, L. 1968. *Human adaptation and its failures*. New York: Academic Press.

Piaget, J. 1951a. *Judgement and reasoning in the child*. London: Routledge and Kegan Paul.

------. 1951b. *Play, dreams, and imitation in childhood*. New York: W. W. Norton.

------. 1952. *The origins of intelligence in children*. New York: International Universities Press.

Pick, H. L., and Pick, A. D. 1970. Sensory and perceptual development. In *Carmichael's manual of child psychology*, edited by P. Mussen. New York: Wiley.

Prescott, E., and Jones, E. 1972. *Day care as a child-rearing environment*, vol. 2. Washington, D. C.: National Association for the Education of Young Children.

Pringle, M. L., and Bossio, V. 1958. A study of deprived children. *Vita Humana* 1: 65-91, 142-169.

Provence, S. 1967. *Guide for the care of infants in groups*. New York: Child Welfare League of America.

------. 1968. The first year of life: The infant. In *Early child care,* edited by L. L. Dittmann. New York: Atherton Presss.

Rabin, A. I., 1958a. Infants and children under conditions of intermittent mothering in the kibbutz. *American Journal of Orthopsychiatry* 28: 577-581.

------. 1958b. Some psychosexual differences between kibbutz and nonkibbutz Israeli boys. *Journal of Projective Techniques* 22: 238-332.

Rank, O. 1929. *The trauma of birth*. New York: Harcourt and Brace.

Rebelsky, F., and Hanks, C. 1972. Fathers' verbal interaction with infants in the first three months of life. *Child Development* 42: 63-68.

Redl, F. 1966. *When we deal with children*. New York: Free Press.

Reese, H. W., and Lipsitt, L. P. 1970. *Experimental child psychology*. New York: Academic Press.

Rheingold, H. L. 1968. Infancy. *Inter-*

national Encyclopedia of the Social Sciences, vol. 7. New York: Crowell-Collier & Macmillan: 224-285.

------. 1971. The social and socializing infant. In *Handbook of socizlization theory and research,* edited by D. A. Goslin. Chicago: Rand-McNally: 779-790.

Rheingold, H. L., and Bayley, N. 1959. The later effects of an experimental modification of mothering. *Child Development* 30: 363-372.

Rheingold, H. L., and Eckerman, C. O. 1973. Fear of the stranger: A critical examination. In *Advances in child development and behavior,* vol. 8, edited by H. W. Reese. New York: Academic Press.

Rheingold, H. L., Gewirtz, J. L., and Ross, H. W. 1959. Social conditioning of vocalizations in the infant. *Journal of Comparative Physiological Psychology* 52: 68-73.

Rheingold, H. L., and Samuels, H. R. 1969. Maintaining the positive behavior of infants by increased stimulation. *Developmental Psychology* 1: 520-527.

Ribble, M. A. 1943. *The rights of infants.* New York: Columbia University Press.

Riesen, A. H. 1961. Stimulation as a requirement for growth and function in behavioral development. In *Functions of varied experience,* edited by D. W. Fiske and S. R. Maddi. Homewood, Ill.: Dorsey.

Ritvo, S., and Solnit, A. 1958. Influence of early mother-child relations in identification. *Psychoanalytic Study of the Child* 13: 64-91.

Robertson, James, and Robertson, Joyce. 1971. Young children in brief separation: A fresh look. *Psychoanalytic Study of the Child* 26: 264-315.

Robinson, H. B., and Robinson, H. M., 1971. Longitudinal development of very young children in a comprehensive day care program: The first two years. *Child Development* 42: 1673-1683.

Robson, K. S. 1967. The role of eye-to-eye contact in maternal-infant attachment. *Journal of Child Psychology and Psychiatry* 8: 13-25.

Robson, K. S., and Moss, H. 1970. Patterns and determinants of maternal attachment. *Journal of Pediatrics* 77: 976-985.

Rosenzweig, M. R. 1966. Environmental complexity, cerebral change, and behavior. *American Scientist* 21: 321-332.

Rousseau, J. J. 1916 (1792). *Emile*. Translated by Barbara Foxley. New York: Everyman's Library.

Rowell, Thelma. 1962. The social development of some rhesus monkeys. In *Determinants of infant behavior,* vol. 2, edited by B. M. Foss. New York: Wiley.

Rubenstein, J. 1967. Maternal attentiveness and subsequent exploratory behavior in the infant. *Child Development* 38: 1089-1100.

Samuels, I. 1959. Reticular mechanisms and behavior. *Psychological Bulletin* 56: 3-25.

Sayegh, Y., and Dennis, W. 1965. The effect of supplementary experiences upon the behavioral development of infants in institutions. *Child Development* 36: 81-90.

Scarr-Salapatek, S., and Williams, M. L. 1973. The effects of early stimulation on low birth-weight infants. *Child Development* 44: 94-101.

Schaefer, E. S. 1965. Configurational analysis of children's reports of parent behavior. *Journal of Consulting Psychology* 29: 552-557.

------. 1972. Parents as educators. In *The Young Child. Review of Research,* vol. 2. Washington, D. C.: National Association for the Education of Young Children.

Schaefer, E. S., and Bayley, N. 1963. Maternal behavior, child behavior, and their inter-correlation from infancy through adolescence. *Monographs of the Society for Research in Child Development 28* (Serial No. 87).

Schaffer, H. R. 1971 Cognitive structure and early social behavior. In *The origins of human social relations,* edited by H. R. Schaffer. New York: Academic Press.

Schaffer, H. R., and Emerson, P. E. 1964. *The development of social attachment in infancy*. Monographs of the Society for Research in Child Development 29 (Serial No. 94).

Schneirla, T. C. 1965. Aspects of stimulation and organization in approach-withdrawal processes underlying vertebrate behavioral development. In *Advances in the study of behavior,* vol. 1, edited by D. S. Lehrman, R. Hinde, and E. Shaw. New York: Academic Press.

Schur, M. 1960. The theory of the parent-infant relationship. *International Journal of Psychoanalysis* 41: 243-245.

Schvaneveldt, J. D. 1964. The development of a film test for the measurement of perceptions toward maternal overprotection. Unpublished doctoral dissertation. Florida State University.

Scott, J. P. 1968. *Early experience and the organization of behavior*. Belmont, Calif.: Brooks/Cole.

Sears, R. R., Maccoby, E. E., and Levin, H. 1957. *Patterns of childrearing*. Evanston, Ill.: Row.

Sears, R. R., and Wise, G. 1950. Relation of cup-feeding in infancy to thumb sucking and the oral drive. *American Journal of Orthopsychiatry* 20: 123-138.

Shirley, M. M. 1933. *The first two years: A study of twenty-five babies,* vol. 2. *Intellectual development*. Child welfare monograph no. 7.

Sigel, I. 1970. The distancing hypothesis: A causal hypothesis for the acquisition of representational thought. In *Miami symposium on the predication of behavior, 1968: Effects of early experience,* edited by M. R. Jones. Coral Gables, Fla.: University of Miami Press.

Sigelman, E. 1969. Reflective and impulsive observing behavior. *Child Development* 40: 1213-1222.

Simsarian, F. 1947. Case histories of five thumb-sucking children breast fed on unscheduled regimes, without limitation of nursing time. *Child Development* 18: 180-184.

Skolnick, A. S., and Skolnick, J. H. 1971. *The family in transition.* Boston: Little, Brown.

Sokolov, E. N. 1960. Neuronal models and the orienting reflex. In *CNS and behavior,* III, edited by A. B. Brazier. New York: Josiah Macy, Jr., Foundation: 187-276.

Solkoff, N., Yaffe, S., Weintraub, D., and Blase, B. 1969. Effects of handling on the subsequent developments of premature infants. *Developmental Psychology* 1: 765-768.

Solnit, A. J. 1969. A study of object loss in infancy. *Psychoanalytic Study of the Child* 25: 257-271.

Sontag, L. W. 1944. War and the fetal maternal relationship. *Marriage and Family Living* 6: 1-5.

------. 1966. Implications of fetal behavior and environment for adult personalities. *Annals of the New York Academy of Sciences* 134: 782-786.

Spears, W. C. 1964. Assessment of visual preference and discrimination in the four-month-old infant. *Journal of Comparative Physiological Psychology* 57: 381-386.

Spears, W. C., and Hohle, R. H. 1967. Sensory and perceptual processes. In *Infancy and early childhood: A handbook and guide to human development,* edited by Y. Brackbill. New York: Free Press.

Sperry, R. W. 1952. Neurology and the mind-brain problem. *American Scientist* 40: 291-312.

------. 1954. On the neural basis of the conditioned response. *The British Journal of Animal Behaviour* 3: 41-44.

Spitz, R. A. 1945. Hospitalism: An inquiry into the genesis of psychiatric conditions in early childhood. *Psychoanalytic Study of the Child* 1: 53-74.

Spitz, R. A. (with the assistance of Wolf, K. M.) 1946a. Anaclitic depression. *Psychoanalytic Study of the Child* 2: 313-342.

------. 1946b. The smiling response: A contribution to the ontogenesis of social relations. *Genetic Psychology Monographs* 34: 57-125.

Spitz, R. A. 1950. Anxiety in infancy: A

study of its manifestations in the
first year of life. *International Journal of Psychoanalysis* 31: 138-143.

------. 1955. The primal cavity: A contribution to the genesis of perception and
its role for psychoanalytic theory.
Psychoanalytic Study of the Child 10:
215-240.

------. 1957. *No and yes: On the genesis
of human communication*. New York: International Universities Press.

------. 1965. *The first year of life*. New
York: International Universities Press.

Stayton, J. D., Hogan, R., and Ainsworth,
M. D. 1971. Infant obedience and maternal behavior: The origins of socialization reconsidered. *Child Development*
42: 1057-1069.

Steinschneider, A., Lipton, E. L., and
Richmond, J. B. 1966. Auditory sensitivity in the infant: Effect of intensity on cardiac and motor responsiv-
ity. *Child Development* 31: 233-252.

Stolz, L. M. 1960. Effects of maternal em-
ployment on children: Evidence from research. *Child Development* 31: 749-782.

Stoner, W. S. 1914. *Natural education*. In-
dianapolis, Ind.: Bobbs-Merrill.

Straub, M. F. 1971. Self-stimulation in
utero. *Psychological Reports* 28: 55-63.

Streissguth, A. P., and Bee, H. 1972.
Mother-child interactions and cognitive

development in children. *Young Children* 154: 173.

Strickland, S. P. 1971. Can slum children learn? *American Education*. Washington, D. C.: U. S. Department of Health, Education, and Welfare: 3-7.

Swift, J. 1964. Effects of early group experience: The nursery school and day nursery. In *A review of child development,* vol. 1, edited by M. Hoffman and L. Hoffman. New York: Russell Sage Foundation: 249-288.

Thomas, A., Chess, S., and Birch, H. 1970. The origin of personality. *Scientific American* 233: 102-109.

Thomas, H. 1965. Visual-fixation responses of infants to stimuli of varying complexity. *Child Development* 36: 629-638.

Thompson, W. R. 1957. Influence of prenatal and maternal anxiety on emotionality of young rats. *Science* 125: 698-699.

Thompson, W. R., and Schaefer, T. 1961. Early environmental stimulation. In *Functions of varied experience,* edited by D. W. Fiske and S. R. Maddi. Homewood, Ill.: Dorsey Press.

Thoreau, H. D. 1962 (1854). *Walden*. New York: Twayne Publishers.

Tronich, E. 1972. Infant day care. Talk given at National Association for the Education of Young Children conference,

Atlanta.

Trosler, G. 1968. The consequences of separation. In *Children in care,* edited by
R. J. N. Tod. London: Longmans, Green.

Tulkin, S. R. 1973. Social class differences in infants' reactions to mother's
and strangers' voices. *Developmental
Psychology* 8: 137.

Tulkin, S. R., and Kagan, J. 1972. Mother-
child interaction in the first year of
life. *Child Development* 42: 31-41.

Vinson, B. W. 1972. Black infant-mother
attachment as related to acquisition of
object person permanence concept. Unpublished doctoral dissertation. Florida State University.

Wachs, T. D., and Cucinotta, P. 1971. The
effect of enriched neonatal experiences
upon later cognitive development. *Developmental Psychology* 5: 542.

Wachs, T. D., Uzgiris, I. C., and Hunt, J.
McV. 1971. Cognitive development in infants of different age levels and from
different environmental backgrounds: An
exploratory investigation. *Merill-Pal-
mer Quarterly* 17: 283-317.

Wahler, R. G. 1967. Infant social attachments: A reinforcement theory: Inter-
pretation and investigation. *Child Development* 38: 1079-1088.

------. 1969. Infant social development:
Some experimental analysis of an infant-mother interaction during the

first year of life. *Journal of Experimental Child Psychology* 7: 101-113.

Walk, R. D., and Gibson, E. J. 1961. *A comparative and analytical study of visual depth perception*. Psychological Monographs 75, no. 15.

Walter, G. W. 1965. Effects on anterior brain responses of an expected association between stimuli. *Journal of Psychosomatic Research* 9: 45-49.

Walters, C. E. 1964. Reliability and comparison of four types of fetal activity and total activity. *Child Development* 35: 1249-1256.

------. 1965. Prediction of postnatal development from fetal activity. *Child Development* 36: 801-808.

------. 1966-71. Effect of fetal activity on apprehension and aggression. National Institute of Mental Health (Behavioral Science Research Branch), R01 MH 12831.

Walters, J., Connor, R., and Zunich, M. 1964. Interaction of mothers and children from lower-class families. *Child Development* 35: 433-440.

Walters, R. H., and Parke, R. D. 1964. Social motivation, dependency, and susceptibility to social influence. In *Advances in experimental social psychology*, vol. 1, edited by L. Berkowitz. New York: Academic Press.

Watson, J. S. 1966. Perception of object orientation in infants. *Merrill-Palmer Quarterly* 12: 73-94.

------. 1971. Cognitive-perceptual development in infancy: Setting for the
   seventies. *Merrill-Palmer Quarterly* 17:
   139-152.

Weikart, D. P., and Lambie, D. Z. 1968.
   Preschool intervention through a home
   teaching program. In *The disadvantaged
   child,* edited by J. Hellmuth. Seattle:
   Special Child Publications 2.

Weil, A. P. 1970. The basic core. *Psychoanalytic Study of the Child* 25: 442-
   460.

Weisberg, P. 1963. Social and nonsocial
   conditioning of infant vocalizations.
   Child Development 34: 377-388.

Wenar, C. G. 1971. *Personality development: From infancy to adulthood.* Boston: Houghton Mifflin.

------. 1972. Executive competence and
   spontaneous social behavior in one-
   year-olds. *Child Development* 43: 256-
   260.

Wender, P. H., Pedersen, F. A., and Waldrop, M. F. 1967. A longitudinal study
   of early social behavior and cognitive
   development. *American Journal of Orthopsychiatry* 37: 691-696.

White, B. L. 1967. An experimental approach to the effects of experiences on
   nearly human behavior. In *Minnesota
   symposium on child psychology,* vol. 1,
   edited by J. P. Hill. Minneapolis:
   University of Minnesota Press.

------. 1969. The initial coordination of sensorimotor schema in human infants: Piaget's ideas and the role of experience. In *Studies in cognitive development,* edited by D. Elkind and J. H. Flavell. New York: Oxford University Press.

------. *Human infants: Experience and psycological development,* vol. 1. Englewood Cliffs, N. J.: Prentice-Hall.

White, B. L., and Castle, P. 1964. Visual exploratory behavior following post-natal handling of human infants. *Perceptual Motor Skills* 18: 497-502.

White, B. L., Castle, P., and Held, R. 1964. Observations on the development of visually directed reaching. *Child Development* 35: 349-364.

White, B. L., and Held, R. 1966. Plasticity of sensorimotor development in the human infant. In *The causes of behavior* (2d ed.), edited by J. F. Rosenblith and W. Allinsmith. Boston: Allyn & Bacon.

White, R. W. 1959. Motivation reconsidered: The concept of competence. *Psychological Review* 66: 297-323.

------. 1962. Competence and the psychosexual stages of development. In *The causes of behavior,* edited by J. F. Rosenblith and W. Allinsmith. Boston: Allyn & Bacon.

Whiting, J. W. M., Landauer, T. K., and Jones, T. M. 1968. Infantile immunization and adult stature. *Child Develop-*

ment 39: 59-67.

Wile, R., and Davis, R. 1941. Relation of birth to behavior. *American Journal of Orthopsychiatry* 11: 320-334.

Winnicott, D. W. 1960. The theory of the parent-child relationship. *International Journal of Psychoanalysis* 41: 585-595.

------. 1965. *The family and individual development*. New York: Basic Books.

Witkin, H. A. 1971. Social influences in the development of cognitive style. In *Handbook of socialization theory and research,* edited by D. A. Goslin. Chicago: Rand McNally.

Wolfenstein, M. 1953. Trends in infant care. *American Journal of Orthopsychiatry* 23: 120-130.

Wolff, P. H. 1963. Observations on the early development of smiling. In *Determinants of infant behavior,* vol. 2, edited by B. M. Foss. New York: Wiley.

Wolins, M. 1963. Some theory and practice in child care: A cross-cultural view. *Child Welfare* 42: 369-377.

------. 1970. Group care: Friend or foe? In *Annual progress in child psychiatry and child development,* edited by S. Chess and A. Thomas. New York: Brunner/Mazel.

World Health Organization. 1964. *Care of*

children in day centers. Geneva: World Health Organization.

Yarrow, L. J. 1954. The relationship of nutritive sucking and experience in infancy and nonnutritive sucking in childhood. *Journal of Genetic Psychology* 84: 149-162.

------. 1961. Maternal deprivation: Toward an empirical and conceptual reevaluation. *Psychological Bulletin* 158: 459-490.

------; 1963. Research in dimensions of early maternal care. *Merrill-Palmer Quarterly* 9: 101-114.

------. 1964. Separation from parents during early childhood. In *Review of child development research,* vol. 1, edited by M. Hoffman and L. Hoffman. New York: Russell Sage Foundation.

------. 1968. The crucial nature of early experience. In *Environmental influences,* edited by D. C. Glass. New York: Rockefeller University and the Russell Sage Foundation.

Yarrow, L. J., Rubenstein, J. L., Pedersen, F. A., and Jankowski, J. J. 1972. Dimensions of early stimulation and their differential effects on infant development. *Merrill-Palmer Quarterly* 18: 205-218.

INDEX OF AUTHORS

INDEX OF SUBJECTS